REFCO

This catalogue is dedicated to the individuals who work at Refco.

The Refco Collection

With an introduction by
Judith Russi Kirshner and essays by
Eleanor Heartney, Anne Rorimer,
and James Yood

Organized by Adam Brooks
Edited by Sue Taylor

Published by
Refco Group, Ltd., Chicago, Illinois

The Refco Collection
Eleanor Heartney, Judith Russi Kirshner, Anne Rorimer, James Yood

Library of Congress Number
90-60227
ISBN 0-9625703-0-3 (pbk.)
ISBN 0-9625703-1-1

Inquiries should be addressed to Refco Group, Ltd.
111 West Jackson
Chicago, Illinois 60604
Attn. Adam Brooks

Cover:
Bruce Nauman
Double Poke in the Eye II, 1985
Neon, aluminum
ed.13/40, 24 x 36 x 6 1/4

Publication design by Donald Bergh, Bergh Jensen & Associates

Photography by Michael Tropea, except pages 44 (left), 88, 104 (left), and 126 by D. James Dee, and page 44 (center), by Steve Elmore.

This book is printed on Lustro Offset Enamel, by Northstar Printing, Minneapolis, Minnesota.

The type is from the Frutiger family, and was composed in Aldus Pagemaker 4.0 on a Macintosh II.

Catalogue dimensions are in inches; height precedes width precedes depth.

Essays are indicated with author's initials:
Eleanor Heartney EH
Anne Rorimer AR
James Yood JY

Contents

6 Acknowledgments
Frances R. Dittmer

8 Introduction
Judith Russi Kirshner

22 Carl Andre
24 John Armleder
26 Richard Artschwager
28 Jo Baer
30 Lothar Baumgarten
32 Bernd and Hilla Becher
34 Lynda Benglis
36 Barbara Bloom
38 Christian Boltanski
40 Richard Bosman
42 Marcel Broodthaers
44 Daniel Buren
46 John Cage
48 John Chamberlain
50 Christo
52 Tony Cragg
54 Carroll Dunham
56 Nancy Dwyer
58 Dan Flavin
60 Günther Förg
62 Gilbert and George
64 Ilona Granet
66 Philip Guston
68 Hans Haacke
70 Peter Halley
72 Eva Hesse
74 Jenny Holzer
76 Rebecca Horn
78 Jim Jacobs
80 Neil Jenney
82 Jasper Johns
84 Donald Judd
86 Anselm Kiefer
88 Komar and Melamid
90 Jeff Koons
92 Willi Kopf
94 Jannis Kounellis
96 Barbara Kruger
98 Annette Lemieux
100 Sherrie Levine
102 Sol LeWitt
104 Donald Lipski
106 Richard Long
108 Mark Luyten
110 Robert Mangold
112 Robert Mapplethorpe
114 Brice Marden
116 Agnes Martin
118 Allan McCollum
120 Robert Morris
122 Bruce Nauman
124 Blinky Palermo
126 Giulio Paolini
128 A. R. Penck
130 Sylvia Plimack-Mangold
132 Sigmar Polke
134 Richard Prince
136 Garnett Puett
138 Martin Puryear
140 Holt Quentel
142 Arnulf Rainer
144 Robert Rauschenberg
146 Richard Rezac
148 Gerhard Richter
150 Tim Rollins and K.O.S.
152 James Rosenquist
154 Ed Ruscha
156 Robert Ryman
158 Italo Scanga
160 Julian Schnabel
162 Sean Scully
164 Carole Seborovski
166 Richard Serra
168 Cindy Sherman
170 Sandy Skoglund
172 Haim Steinbach
174 Frank Stella
176 Donald Sultan
178 Tony Tasset
180 Andy Warhol
182 William Wegman
184 Christopher Wilmarth
186 Bill Woodrow

190 The Refco Collection

Acknowledgments

The development of the Refco Collection has involved many talented and generous people. Thanking the following contributors here is only the formal acknowledgment of my immeasurable gratitude and appreciation:

To the artists represented in the collection, whose work reflects concerns and developments in art of the past thirty years, and continues to be a source of challenge, wonder, and enlightenment.

To Thomas Dittmer, Tone Grant, and Phillip Bennett, the principal officers of Refco, whose unwavering commitment and unqualified encouragement made the collection possible.

To Rhona Hoffman for her deep involvement and commitment to the collection. She has been a profound source of inspiration, an invaluable resource of education, and a major influence in shaping the aesthetic standards of the collection.

To Brooke Alexander and Bill Van Straaten for their early assistance in acquiring prints and multiples, which formed the basis of the collection in the 1970s.

To the following art dealers and gallery personnel for their generous assistance and involvement with the collection:

Ted Bonin, Brooke Alexander, Inc., New York City; Anthony d'Offay and Glenn McMillan, Anthony d'Offay Gallery, London; Hudson, Feature Gallery, New York City; Frances Beatty and Lance Kinz, Richard L. Feigen & Co., New York City and Chicago; Marian Goodman and Jill Sussman-Walla, Marian Goodman Gallery, New York City; Donald McKinney and Betty Cunningham, Hirschl & Adler Modern, New York City; Dennis Nielson, Susan Reynolds, Bradford Trayser and Grace Weiss, Rhona Hoffman Gallery, Chicago; Marianne Holterman, London; Robbin Lockett, Robbin Lockett Gallery, Chicago; Bob Monk and Susan Lorence, Lorence-Monk Gallery, New York City; Joshua Mack, New York City; Douglas Baxter and Peter Boris, The Pace Gallery, New York City; John Weber, Joyce Nereaux, and Thomas Schulte, John Weber Gallery, New York City; Donald Young, Barbara Mirecki, and Michael Hill, Donald Young Gallery, Chicago.

To the many other art dealers, too numerous to mention here, who have provided works of art to the collection and have been significant sources of ideas, knowledge, and information.

In the preparation and publication of this catalogue, I have been privileged to work with several exceptionally gifted people. My great admiration and immense gratitude to the following:

To Judith Russi Kirshner for her insightful and enlightening introduction to this catalogue.

To James Yood and Eleanor Heartney for their cogent and instructive essays on the works of art featured in the catalogue, and to Anne Rorimer for her perceptive essay on the Daniel Buren installation.

To Michael Tropea, for his exemplary photography of the collection.

To Sue Taylor for her unflagging editorial assistance, and to Paula Hoffman for her thorough proofreading.

To Donald Bergh, of Bergh Jensen & Associates, for his cooperation and talented publication design efforts in our behalf.

And finally, my deepest and heartfelt appreciation to my Associate Curator, Adam Brooks, for his support and collaboration in developing the Refco Collection and for his stewardship in the preparation of this catalogue.

Frances R. Dittmer

Introduction

Judith Russi Kirshner

Corporate patronage of the arts has deep roots in Renaissance Italy, where wealthy bankers and merchants began to invest substantial sums in culture. Building vast collections as well as imposing reputations, the Medici and Strozzi families of Florence became legendary models of artistic patronage. Additionally, guilds and religious confraternities dedicated significant resources to the construction of what are now considered great monuments of Western art. The motivations of Renaissance collectors were widely disparate, dependent on economic circumstances and individual aesthetic choice informed by cultural developments. As patrons of ecclesiastical projects, donors sought to assuage their consciences for questionable commercial activities and hoped that their munificence might bring rewards in the afterlife. Others financed major building programs to legitimize and give material expression to their political and cultural leadership in the community. Finally there were, and continue to be, the pleasures attached to the ownership of aesthetic objects, and the gratification of playing a primary role in the elaborate processes of artistic creation and reception.

Stated or unstated, motivations for collecting art from the Renaissance to the present remain fluid and varied. So too are the myriad varieties of patronage. Private collections have become public on certain occasions, as they are often lent, donated, or sold to public institutions. Recently in the United States, private foundations have been formed to acquire, display, and lend works of art. Individual private collections have overlapped with corporate collections; they may be temporary or permanent. In the market system, where support of artists is often indirect and anonymous, a client, individual or corporate, typically purchases a work of art without ever encountering the artist. By contrast, in a commission, a patron selects an artist to create a work for a particular circumstance or setting, perpetuating practices now more than five centuries old.

Fifteen years ago, Frances Dittmer, wife of the founder and chairman of the board of Refco, began acquiring graphic works for the rapidly expanding futures trading firm formed in 1969 in Chicago, where it still has its home office. This early acquisition of prints by Jasper Johns—*First Etchings* (1967-68), *Grey Alphabet* (1968), *Decoy* (1971), and *Land's End* (1979)—immediately announced an ambitious commitment which has been borne out continually through the development of this collection of 280 contemporary paintings, sculpture, graphics, and installation work. Now the largest commodities brokerage house in the world, Refco has established a reputation for its emphasis on educating clients and risk-taking in investment strategies. With offices in twenty-eight cities in Europe and the United States, Refco presents its art collection in New York and Chicago to a primary audience of six hundred employees and numerous clients who interact with the art daily in the corporate environment.

In the twentieth century, a surge of interest in corporate collecting accompanied the rise of Abstract Expressionism as a distinctively American variant of Modernism after the Second World War. In order to advance a vision of America through its culture, partnerships between art and industry were constructed. Abstract Expressionism, although seemingly without apparent referents and lacking overt representational qualities, quickly came to represent innovation and American virtue; it was energetic, ambitious in content, and large in scale. When pop artists working in the sixties abandoned brushstroke and gesture for already existent images of popular culture and mass-produced objects as a provocative means for artistic expression, another chapter of exchange between business and culture was underway, seen for example in the large canvases of James Rosenquist, the puns of Ed Ruscha, and brand names of Andy Warhol. At the same time, brightly hued, large-scale color-field painting and streamlined steel sculpture became accessories for high-tech offices and lobbies.

Instead of the commercial imagery of popular culture, minimalist artists in the late sixties used geometry, technological methods, and industrial materials in the manufacture of their art objects. Some of the most direct statements of Minimalism's aims were articulated by the artists themselves, among them Donald Judd. His 1965 essay "Specific Objects" set the terms for a minimalist focus on art that was simple, clear, and literal. In some cases, this attitude was inspired by avant-garde composer John Cage and artists like Johns and Robert Rauschenberg, also represented in this collection, whose art was sometimes dictated by chance occurrences and fueled by the contingencies of its material environment. Often minimalist art utilized scale as content, denied reference to anything beyond itself, and insisted that less is more.

Richard Artschwager's *Diptych #3* (1967) straddles tenets of pop humor and minimal muteness. Combining the most utilitarian and banal material—formica—with a format associated with conventional painting, the artist has produced an ironic object with wood-patterned wings that suggest shutters framing a central void, a blank. In the even more reduced and elegant examples of Judd and Carl Andre, sculpture either hangs on the wall or rests on the floor, contradicting the anthropomorphic implications of traditional sculpture, usually vertical and upright. Fabricated from steel elements, these works make it immediately obvious that everything unessential has been removed, that repetition of similar units has replaced composition in rhythmic structures, and finally that literal space is more important than depicted space.

This work almost always denies formalism (that is, form for form's sake), expression, and, in the case of Dan Flavin's construction, even dematerializes its support as fluorescent modules cast an aura of color that appears to melt the wall. In Andre's aluminum-copper alloy carpet, sculpture as place, neither form nor structure, demonstrates how minimalist art called upon viewers to apprehend another definition of sculptural space. At first the work may appear visually austere, yet the experience can become rich and varied as one passes across the hundred squares of Andre's work and contemplates the tension and compression of this sculptural conception. By the same token, the repeated delicate folds of steel in Judd's series *Untitled (3 Folded Meters)* (1971) reveal the subtle rewards of an intelligible system extended in a visible sequence.

Still an influential movement twenty years later, Minimalism appeared to be difficult for collectors when it was first exhibited, as much because of its visual sparseness as because of its theoretical underpinnings. According to Mel Bochner, another artist associated with Minimalism, "Old Art attempted to make the non-visible (energy/feeling) visual (marks). The New Art is attempting to make the non-visual (mathematics) visible (concrete)."[1] Even though we might consider these two polarities as overly simple, it is nonetheless at these points that many artists and collectors part company. In the Refco Collection, this generation of artists, whose blunt, unromantic aesthetic positions held little appeal for some audiences, is represented in unusual depth: from the dusky tints of Sol LeWitt's wall drawing *Multiple Asymmetrical Pyramids* (1987), whose cones appear like canopies behind the furniture in the entrance to the New York office, to the dazzling bars of Peter Halley's canvas *Prison with Yellow Background* (1984), one can span the depth of influence this movement has maintained and rediscover its elegance and cerebral pleasures.

A major artist who began his career in the late sixties with a minimal and conceptual vocabulary and non-organic forms, LeWitt is famous for his sculptures based on grids and finite progressive systems as well as for his wall drawings. These latter site-specific works are executed by other draftsmen who transform simple systems into complex fields of line and color applied directly to the wall. LeWitt has composed a brilliant visual score from permutations, rotations, and reversals of a very basic, even constricted vocabulary of geometric shapes. Admiring the experiments of the Russian Constructivists of the early twentieth century, artists like LeWitt and Frank Stella create a visual grammar of things the mind already knows—cubes, squares, lines, and circles.

Painters such as Agnes Martin, Jo Baer, and Robert Ryman also have produced canvases in which aesthetic pleasure is not immediately given up but comes through contemplation. Martin's exquisitely subtle art is represented here by a composition that seems to be a scrim of delicate color over a foundation of a modernist grid. Ryman has relied on material and procedural essentials—canvas, white pigment, and hardware supports—to generate paintings whose variations and effects are as multiple as their means are limited. For Ryman, each choice is crucial: the color and texture of the support, whether linen, wood, or metal; the kind of pigment; the size and direction of the brushstroke. Each work of art thus becomes a definition, demonstration, and example of the mystery that occurs in the process of artistic manipulation.

While many critics in the eighties considered the resurgence of Neo-Expressionism—exemplified in this collection by Richard Bosman's thickly painted scenes of peril as well as works by Anselm Kiefer and Julian Schnabel—as a reaction against the severities of Minimalism, its conceptual programs continue to induce new interpretations by artists like Halley and sculptor Tony Tasset. Tasset literally domesticates some of Minimalism's hard edges, using sensuous materials such as fur and leather. Halley, referring to color-field paintings by artists such as Barnett Newman, translates Day-Glo hues from the everyday environment into geometric patterns that suggest prisons and circuits. Influenced by European theoreticians, Halley, like his minimalist predecessors, is a gifted critic; his writing depends on postmodern sources that question the concepts of tradition and originality.

Another influential artist and critic is Robert Morris, whose work has spanned two decades and several styles, including Minimalism and Postminimalism. In a drawing from the series *Blind Time* (1985), Morris investigated his own creative capacities under the constraint of a blindfold and limited time—seven minutes. What remains are the gestures and traces of his movements across the page. Sculptor's drawings constitute a particularly fascinating field, and the dense, impenetrable sheet by Richard Serra approximates the weight and gravity of his steel constructions. One of the very remarkable works in the collection is a wall sculpture by Eva Hesse, whose premature death in 1970 limited her oeuvre but not her influence and importance as one of the first postminimalist artists.

A contemporary and friend of LeWitt, Hesse personalized and experimented with the possibilities offered by Minimalism. She also chose repetition and sequences of circles and squares as her subject matter, yet her forms proliferate to become communities and are transformed as they are translated into soft and often transparent materials. Hesse's resin *Sans II* (1968), a segment of one of her most ambitious pieces, is golden; its wrinkled units literally catch light like a painting yet hold it like sculpture; the geometric progression is simultaneously a pliable container and series of windows. Lynda Benglis's early, postminimal sculptures of poured latex were monstrous extrusions mounted on the wall; she has continued to combine sinuous contours with gorgeous surfaces—in this case, wall-mounted gold knots whose torsion suggests anatomical forms. Hinting at vaguely anthropological functions, Martin Puryear has wedded the lessons of minimalist economy to natural materials to produce sculpture that remains mysterious and so beautifully crafted that his artistry is almost invisible.

During the past decade, the art world embraced revisions and revivals of earlier models in a multiplicity of approaches variously linked together by the hotly debated term Postmodernism. First used to describe the return to classical forms and ornamentation in architecture, Postmodernism signaled a deeper rejection of the unfulfilled promises of Modernism, that is, of progress through abstraction and the avant garde. Inspired by analytical techniques of literary criticism, Marxism, and feminism, many artists and critics abandoned the expression of intuition and emotion for the arena of critical theory. With little belief left in the possibility of true originality or an identifiable point of reference, there was a sometimes cynical resignation to the power of reproduction and consumerism as determining factors of creation.

One encounters in the Refco Collection some of the major artists of the eighties who often question the assumptions of the very styles they embrace. Indeed this spirit of inquiry, of analyzing rather than accepting the givens of any stylistic allegiance or ideology—abstract or representational, conceptual or expressionistic—is a characteristic of many of the artworks in the collection. One of the most discomforting challenges to received notions of art history and particularly the idea of authenticity, has been illustrated in the work of women artists such as Sherrie Levine, who began her career making photographic copies of famous photographs, thereby contesting the power of the original masterpiece. In the Refco Collection, she is represented by a painting on lead patterned like a backgammon board to suggest possibilities of generic abstraction or authorless chance.

Perhaps the most exciting reversal of the eighties was the triumphant re-entry and reception of European artists into the mainstream of the American art world. After the Venice Biennale of 1980, in which many of these artists were first shown to international audiences, Americans were able to appreciate turbulent canvases by German Neo-Expressionists such as Georg Baselitz and A. R. Penck, as well as Kiefer, whose paintings made with lead, sand, and straw assume Wagnerian proportions. From Italy came painters Francesco Clemente, Sandro Chia, and Enzo Cucchi, all of whom became instant celebrities, leading American collectors away from isolationism. Simultaneously, American painters such as David Salle, Schnabel, and Eric Fischl received international acclaim. Giant international exhibitions, self-consciously titled *A New Spirit in Painting* (London, 1981) and *Zeitgeist* (West Berlin, 1982), brought together artists and collectors from many countries, and broadcast a renewed vigor in the heroic possibilities of painting.

With this wave came a revived appreciation for the late figurative and often autobiographical paintings of Philip Guston, earlier renowned as an Abstract Expressionist. His fragmentary images of limbs, piles of shoes, and bottles are admired for their ability to be personal tokens and still speak to larger issues of human self-destruction, the frustrations of creativity, and the plight of the solitary artist. Schnabel, who arrived in New York from Texas, quickly came to exemplify the heroic artist, lionized by the media; his oversize operatic paintings can be studded with pottery shards or painted on velvet. In the Refco Collection, Schnabel's quick, bold marks are applied to maps from Italian touring guides as if to suggest the global range of creativity and the location of his own ambition in the antique world.

Although much of the excitement of the past decade was sensational and occasionally superficial, what remained of these exchanges was the significance of European mentors such as Joseph Beuys, a conceptual artist, teacher, and guru figure, who not only taught many of the new Expressionists in Germany but whose influence can be seen in the art of Schnabel and many younger artists such as the German Günther Förg. Another prophetic figure from Germany is Sigmar Polke;

his paintings fabricated from bits of cloth and stamped with cartoon imagery are often as cryptic as the poisonous-looking materials he uses to compose them. Gerhard Richter's visually stunning abstract expressionist paintings operate on multiple levels. At first glance, they read as gorgeous dramatic compositions, but they are not actually painted; rather, thick swaths are strategically applied to represent the look of mighty gesture. Embracing many styles, Richter consistently incorporates a critical consciousness into the process of painting that renders the possibility of personal expression problematic.

In Italy, Jannis Kounellis, a sculptor associated with the *Arte Povera* (Poor Art) movement in which artists used humble materials indigenous to and evocative of their environment, has been a major force since the early seventies. His remarkable constructions, often enormous walls built from remnants of steel, wood, and broken statuary, demonstrate the burdens and weight of the heritage of ancient cultures. Installed near the rough-hewn, untitled work by Kounellis, Giulio Paolini's white plaster torsos, copies of classical statuary, quote from historical sources and serve as poignant, beautiful reminders of exhausted possibilities. An attempt to understand the loss of millions of victims of the Second World War underlies the power of French artist Christian Boltanski's photographic icons. These electrically illuminated assemblages constitute anonymous memorials or shrines to individuals who not only lost their lives but also their identities and histories.

In a series of black-and-white photographs arranged in grids and categorized according to function and form, the German artists Bernd and Hilla Becher have documented the industrial landscape of Europe and America. Grouped to underscore similarities and differences, these typologies—archaic factories, silos, or in this case water towers—fulfill an archival impulse to record and classify what is being destroyed or forgotten. A more pastoral conception of landscape, distant from industrial monuments and closer to the archaeology of ancient ones, occurs in the subtle and romantic work of Englishman Richard Long. Since 1967, Long has documented his perambulations by leaving marks from local materials—a sculpture at Mount Kilimanjaro, a pattern of ashes in the form of a ziggurat in Peru. On other occasions, the artwork has consisted of modest descriptions of ambitious treks, for example, the 164-mile *Walk across Ireland, Placing a Nearby Stone on My Path at Every Mile along the Journey* (1974). Often composed of stones or wood from the area where the walk is made, Long's art can be arranged in spirals on the gallery or museum floor, or can be exhibited on the wall in photographs, maps, or drawings of the places he has been. In this case, he uses mud from a particular site to document the landscape in strange and handsome sheets where footprints replace the traditional gestural traces of the artist's brush.

Unorthodox materials and reuse of detritus seem particularly pregnant means in the hands of both European and American artists. *Dining Motions* (1988) by Englishman Tony Cragg is constructed from discarded wooden fragments collected by the artist, then reassembled in a jigsaw-puzzle pattern of table utensils enlarged to gigantic proportions on the wall. Also in England, Bill Woodrow literally cuts up metal objects to deny their visible function but transforms them wittily into something else—art. In contrast, John Chamberlain's crushed auto parts are reconstituted into intriguing abstract objects. They demand our attention not only because of their formal power but as insistent reminders of the pervasiveness of American automobile culture. Lessons of ecology and aesthetic reuse are explored more lyrically in Donald Lipski's enormously inventive installations that recall the radical inversions of Marcel Duchamp, the great conceptual artist of the twentieth century. Hounding old factories or warehouses for raw material, Lipski bends, twists, and combines unlikely items together to form poetic objects. All of these bits and pieces are then arranged like three-dimensional equivalents to drawings or personal notations. They also demonstrate how magically the mundane—paper clips, matches—becomes mysterious in the imagination of the artist who orchestrates their placement on the wall.

While some artists turned toward Expressionism as a mode of reaffirming subjectivity and reinvigorating painting, others veered away from handicraft to manipulate the photographic procedures, language, and look of the media—what they considered "real life." Thus, a younger generation of American artists has dealt directly with issues of power in the political and aesthetic realm. Cindy Sherman, for instance, has documented herself in a series of richly staged photos which feature the artist in various costumes: as film-noir movie star, distraught fairy tale heroine, fashion model, and, more recently, figures from historical portraiture. Not only has she shown how powerful are the conventions to which women conform, but also how influential their media representation has become. Difficult to label, this work is more self-fashioning than self-portraiture, a theater of multiple personas both subject and object, cast from feminine poses and positions.

Jeff Koons's glamorous self-promotion through a series of stunning advertisements posed the artist as star surrounded by women in absurdly exotic settings.

In brilliant and cynical amalgams of pop celebrity and advertising techniques, he has elevated kitsch subjects (such as banal knick-knacks and figurines of Michael Jackson, a personal hero for Koons and an individual who also recreated himself), into precious materials and high-art status. A former Wall Street broker, Koons utilized industrial products like pristine vacuum cleaners in his earlier sculpture to provoke questions about the convergence of art and commodity. Negotiating more overtly between these realms is the stylish sculpture of Haim Steinbach, who displays manufactured products on minimal-style shelves or supports.

Animated by the aesthetic inheritance of Warhol, Claes Oldenburg, and Stella, artists of the eighties explored both the farthest shores of personal expression and the choppy waters of consumerism and media barrage. Adopting the graphic style and format of fifties advertising, Barbara Kruger has added colors and photomontage techniques associated with Soviet avant-garde artists to produce images of stunning power about the abuse of power. In *Your Every Wish Is Our Command* (1982), the black-and-white photo of a baby's hand grasping an adult's demonstrates the unequal balance of power and the ambiguities of desire and control. Calling on audiences who respond to images not only for aesthetic reasons but also according to gender, Kruger and Jenny Holzer, and indeed many of the artists in this collection, work with language as a prime element in their art. In this respect, they are following the earlier linguistic investigations of Conceptualists like Dan Graham and Joseph Kosuth.

Although the first chapters of organized feminism coincided with the political uprisings of the late sixties and early seventies, many women artists in the eighties began to use language in art that was pointedly personal...and political. The first woman artist to represent the United States at the Venice Biennale, Holzer has understood how to take spectacular advantage of the boundary dissolution between high and low culture, a significant characteristic of postmodern art. She has moved from urban graffiti and street-art multiples, plastering *Truisms* (1977-79) on city walls, to messages in the urgent *Survival Series* (1983-85) engraved in stone to become memorials that carry troubling narratives of war and violence. These signs are openly critical and speak to concerns of social justice, of psychological as well as political exploitation. *Truisms*, alphabetically organized one-liners such as "Abuse of power comes as no surprise," "Fathers often use too much force," and "Money creates taste," have appeared on T-shirts, on the Spectacolor board of Times Square, and of course on museum walls.

Seizing the potential of the printed format utilized by earlier conceptual artists, Holzer constructs her vernacular statements in clear language that flashes quickly past individuals accustomed to reacting, or not reacting, to a constant bombardment of media messages. She has attributed her attraction to electronic signs and high-technology to their capacity to deliver information efficiently and powerfully. With her *Truisms*, she has attempted "to speak about important things, in places where people can see them and... are going to get it."[2] Holzer's sensitivity to the nuances of everyday aphorism can be compared with the direct language of sculptor Bruce Nauman, another influential artist whose work has involved neon signage since the late 1960s.

Debates on the possibility that artistic expression might extend beyond the confines of museum or collection to comment on or even effect social or political practice are still viable. In Europe, there is a historical tradition of politically engaged art that includes the Russian Constructivists before the Revolution of 1917 and, more recently, artists such as the collaborative team of Vitali Komar and Aleksandr Melamid. Komar and Melamid fled Russia and the constraints of social realism for Israel in 1977, and now live and work in New York and Jersey City, respectively. Their irreverent collaboration includes several invented Russian artists whose facile imitations of nineteenth-century realism are almost eerily convincing in their stylistic correctness, yet defiantly oppositional in their subject matter. In a gorgeous painting whose impact seems stronger now after the extraordinary changes of perestroika, a couple find each other under a portrait of Joseph Stalin, whose political demise has finally been sealed by the democratic revolutions of 1989 and 1990.

Marcel Broodthaers died in Belgium before receiving the acclaim he deserved for his highly idiosyncratic, poetic oeuvre of untraditional materials and linguistic expression, represented in the Refco Collection by *Museum–Museum* (1972). In this double panel, the names of famous artists are conflated and equated with material goods like butter and bacon, and act as labels for images of gold bricks. While Broodthaers negotiated between leftist and art-world politics, some artists have questioned the mechanisms by which patronage extends to become control. Hans Haacke's *Alcoa: We Can't Wait for Tomorrow* (1979) presents a quotation from a former chairman of the company: "Business could hold art exhibitions to tell its own story." Haacke, born in Germany in 1936, has consistently found his subject matter in the connections among economic, political, and cultural practices, using his art to examine the operations of corporations like Alcoa and Mobil as well as those of European mega-collectors like Charles Saatchi and Peter Ludwig.

Haacke's uncompromising installations depend on the time and space in which they are exhibited, and his inclusion here introduces an element of self-consciousness and self-criticism into the Refco Collection. Also of special interest in this collection are site-specific installations, that is, works conceived, designed, and installed according to the givens, both architectural and functional, of a particular situation. Commissioned by Refco, these artworks depend on both a literal and metaphorical support system. Although historians have pointed to early Modernists such as the Futurists in Italy and artists associated with the Bauhaus in Germany as precursors, installations have provided an ongoing challenge to contemporary artists. Already noted in this collection, for example, are the witty accumulations of discarded objects by Lipski and found remnants by Cragg.

Influenced by earlier generations of conceptual artists, American Allan McCollum observes the patterns of production, collection, and installation and how those processes give meaning to and affect our understanding of art. His *Surrogates* (1978-), a series of almost identical objects, look like small framed paintings but are actually cast from plaster. Their centers are blank and black; the dimensions, size of frame, and border are the only variables resulting in art that resembles but never represents. Like the work of Warhol, Koons, and even Holzer, McCollum's series is potentially endless (he has produced about five thousand generic objects) and therefore critical of the tradition that celebrates unique works of art. Extremely handsome when installed, the *Surrogates* can be arranged in any pattern to conform to any situation, like the ubiquitous canvas over the sofa; they heighten our awareness of how we make aesthetic choices and assign aesthetic value.

For more than two decades, French artist Daniel Buren has established an international reputation and has managed to sensitize and educate audiences to the importance of context, to the ways in which we are conditioned to respond to art. Buren always begins with stripes, alternating white and a color printed on canvas or paper. His influential, often impermanent installations of these stripes have taught us how a specific setting, whether the architecture and function of a museum or a trading room, defines and determines our experience of the work of art. Rarely in a museum do we challenge the authority of a given masterpiece, for example, but when in 1972 Buren replaced the paintings in a gallery at Documenta V in Kassel, West Germany, with his striped panels, the modern convention of hanging paintings at the same low level became apparent and predictable. In Chicago in 1981, Buren attached his striped panels to the doors of Illinois Central trains whose progress past the Art Institute's windows invited spectators to look outside the museum to watch the art speed by. Obvious questions such as the limits of art were posed, as were equally provocative problems of understanding contemporary expression: can art ever exist apart from approved institutional support and ideology?

Buren's first U.S. commission for a private corporation, the grandly scaled installation in the Refco trading room in New York enlarges our perceptions and definitions of art. Here, striped panels attached to columns and piers appear like joyous awnings between rather than on the windows. The stripes are rainbow colors or shiny silver; the reflective stripes mirror architectural details in the room and punch out spaces between the windows so that art becomes the frame for breathtaking views of the city. Like some Minimalists, but with a more acute sense of paradox, Buren resists the personality of individual gesture or expression at the same time that his stripes inevitably have become his signature. By now they represent art whether they appear in contexts such as this one, on sails or bridges, or on the white walls of hushed galleries.

For hundreds of years, scholars and philosophers have debated the role of art in society; its purposes have been seen as pleasure, decoration, or as rarified edification usually far removed from the exigencies of daily life. In the last decade, art itself has become a global business, making headlines as auction prices set dizzying records and investors become as multinational as the aesthetic patrimony they acquire. Museums in the seventies turned increasingly to corporations to finance enormous block-buster exhibitions; the impact such economic support might have on curatorial procedures and even artistic choices has not yet been fully addressed. At the same time, contemporary artists have struggled to bring their work back into the arena of engagement, to participate actively in the debates and partnerships between business and culture, to assume that social and political questions can be confronted within the framework of artistic expression.

In the United States and Europe, many artists have worked against the separation between art and life, merging aesthetic goals with social awareness in their work. And it is this kind of challenging, conceptual work that is included in the Refco Collection, with the expectation that the art will in turn intrigue and educate the audiences who view and experience it. Refco's patronage, a partnership of business and culture, is poised between the individual and the corporation, appealing to responses that are both personal and public. By supporting the work of established artists as well as those who are dedicated to the analysis of the establishment, the collection provides an unexpected showcase for art communicated through words and images, neon and pigment, art that stimulates the intellect at the same time that it excites and delights the eye. This catalogue is intended to illustrate some of the significant contributions of these artists, in a collection that constitutes a growing resource for our appreciation and understanding of the vitality of contemporary art.

Notes

[1]Mel Bochner, "Primary Structures: A Declaration of a New Attitude Is Revealed by an Important Current Exhibition," *Arts Magazine* 40:8 (June 1966): 34.

[2]Jenny Holzer, "Wordsmith: An Interview with Jenny Holzer by Bruce Ferguson," in *Jenny Holzer: Signs* (Des Moines, Iowa: Des Moines Art Center, 1986), 74.

Carl **Andre**

1
Aluminum-Copper Alloy Square, 1969
Aluminum, copper; one hundred units
each 1/4 x 7 7/8 x 7 7/8,
1/4 x 78 3/4 x 78 3/4 overall

Carl Andre, born Quincy, Massachusetts, 1935; lives in New York City

It might be surprising to argue that a metal carpet rising less than one-half inch off the floor could constitute an assault on the tradition of sculpture, but that would be a good way to begin to consider the function of *Aluminum-Copper Alloy Square* by Carl Andre. In his floor pieces of the late 1960s, Andre undermined the conventional appearance and silhouette of sculpture, and set in motion intriguing challenges to our own role as observers of art. His artworks sit—or rather, lie—in the last place we might expect to find sculpture, and present us with no subject, image, or referential gesture with which to begin a dialogue. In lieu of those things, Andre's sculpture offers viewers an almost theatrical interactive encounter, a context in which we, not it, begin to take a crucial and central role.

Aluminum-Copper Alloy Square is made up, as its title indicates, of fifty copper and fifty aluminum plates set in a checkerboard pattern. The individual squares are machine cut and rough edged, and not buffed to any great degree of gloss. Almost immediately, we surmise that it would be all right if we were to walk on this sculpture, and in that realization we sense an odd kind of permission to interact with a work of art in a manner that is normally forbidden. There is a charge of pleasure in this encounter, and for a few private moments we are in the art, above and upon the art, in complete possession of it and conscious perhaps even of a bit of secret titillation in degrading it with the soles of our shoes. The contour of the sculpture is not fixed; we can adjust the metal tiles with our feet and note inconsistencies in its awkward and somewhat battered grid.

Of course, it is Andre who orchestrates this range of possibilities, and it is quite probable that he would welcome the curious and variegated scenarios that we experience in response to his work. Although his art is associated with the minimalist movement, that categorization should not be construed to suggest that his ambitions are not multiple and complex. He—and the artists with whom he is often linked, including Donald Judd, Dan Flavin, Robert Morris, and Sol LeWitt—have sought to do no less than revitalize the craft of sculpture by making its interaction with viewers carry primary meaning. Andre's metal grid engages us, demands our participation, awaits our arrival, and, even if we may not admire it, we cannot ignore it. JY

John **Armleder**

Balancing on the cusp between seriousness and parody, the work of Swiss artist John Armleder poses a challenge to ordinary assumptions about the meaning of art. His works offer juxtapositions of everyday functional objects and simple geometric paintings. He may, for instance, place a pair of gleaming new electric guitars alongside a monochrome canvas, ornament an elegant walnut vanity with a painted panel that recalls the compositions of the Russian Constructivists, or, as here, set a minimalist painting next to a Levolor blind.

In these arrangements, the meanings of both elements are changed. We begin to consider, for instance, how compatible the clean horizontal lines of the blind are with the streamlined aesthetic of Minimalism, and how easily the painting becomes a design element within a larger decorative scheme. We realize, in other words, that Armleder has leveled the supposedly sacred hierarchy of art over design, in the process violating the once sovereign autonomy of the aesthetic realm.

Armleder's attack on the "purity" of art has roots in art history. His work makes reference to the fact that in the early twentieth century, abstract art was seen as part of a larger social and cultural program. For artists involved with such movements as Russian Constructivism, de Stijl, and the German Bauhaus, abstract art and avant-garde design were seen as tools with which to remake the world. Only later, in the second half of our century, did abstract art become detached from life, relegated to its own inviolable world.

However, while Armleder rejoins art and design, his work seems too tongue-in-cheek to be a genuine continuation of the ideals of early Modernism. Instead, he plays with the contradictions inherent in our definitions of art. Which, he asks us slyly, is more beautiful: his rather banal abstract compositions or the slick streamlined products of contemporary consumer culture? Which more clearly expresses the essence of contemporary reality? Thus, Armleder resurrects the almost moribund tradition of geometric abstraction not so much to praise it as to bury it. In this he shares the conviction of a number of contemporary artists that the optimism of that earlier era was misplaced. Belief in progress and trust in the ideals of truth, purity, and beauty, he suggests, are as anachronistic as the abstract paintings in his artistic arrangements. EH

2
Untitled, 1987
Oil on canvas with venetian blind
78 3/4 x 67

John Armleder, born Geneva, 1948; lives in Geneva

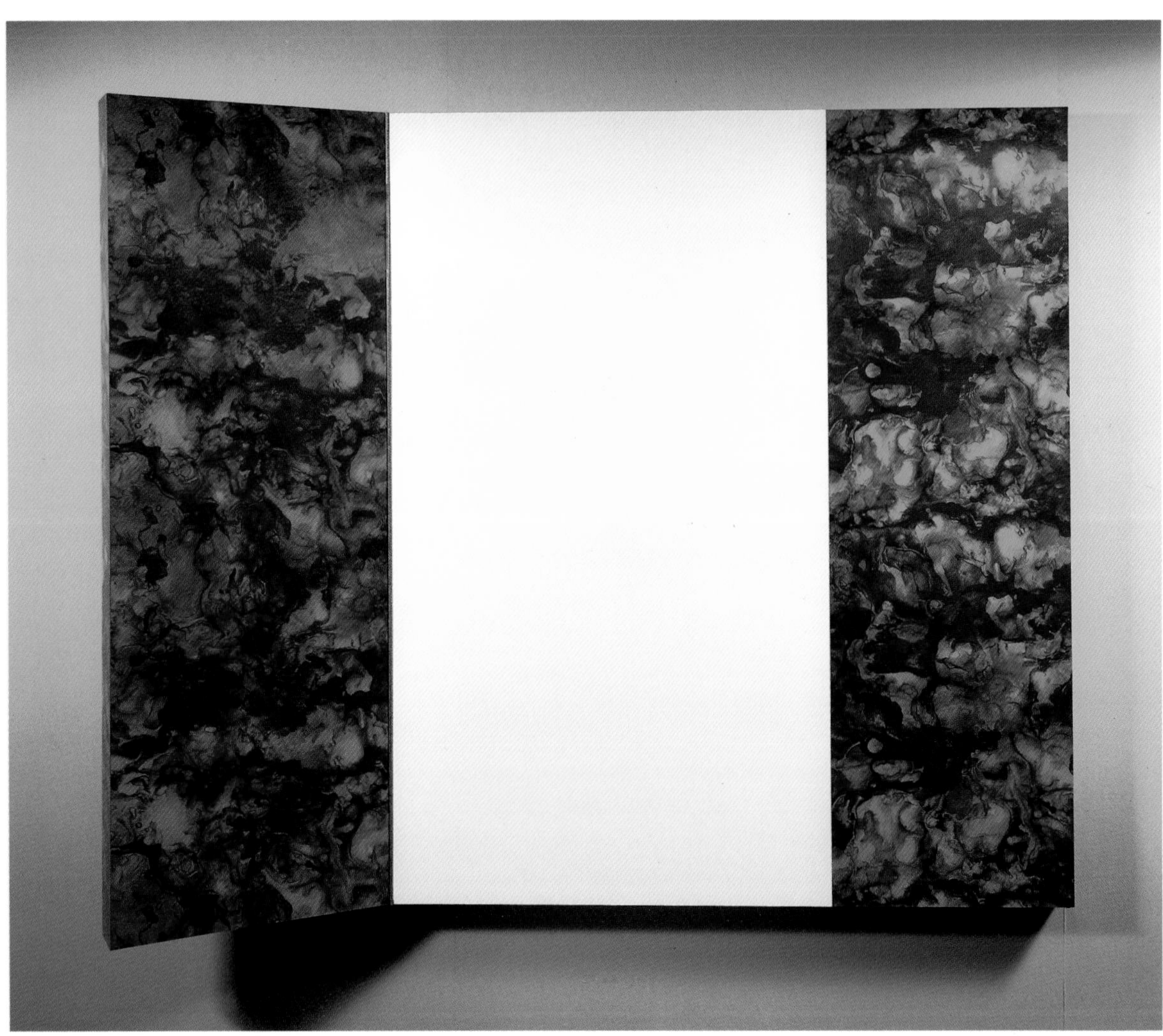

Richard **Artschwager**

Richard Artschwager served a long and varied apprenticeship on his way to becoming an artist. By the time of his first one-person exhibition in 1965, when he was forty-one years old, he had been a soldier, a science student at Cornell University, a baby photographer, bank clerk, lathe operator, and furniture maker. The stops Artschwager made along his way to art did more than merely season him; they had their impact on his fresh and quizzical way of seeing, and left ringing echoes in his art of wit and scrupulous craftsmanship.

Diptych #3 is a subtle smile, an object that seems ready to tell its secrets right out in the open. It is indeed a diptych, a two-panel wall piece made out of a rather garish formica. The hinged section on the left can swing out into our space, allowing us to alter *Diptych #3's* silhouette at will. The rather stolid (even in formica) arrangement of brown-white-brown is simple and austere, and raises a suggestion of religious sources; the object is an alterable altar. In its pristine presentation, this wall sculpture is also reminiscent of minimalist models by artists such as Donald Judd and Carl Andre. But soon the questions, slight ambiguities, and inconsistencies begin to protrude, denying any single satisfying reading of *Diptych #3.*

Although it is physically a diptych, for example, its three-part pictorial structure is that of a triptych; the "wing" on the right seems frozen to the central panel, stuck against its will, permanently fixed to the wall. And for what purpose is Artschwager using the vocabulary of altarpieces for a blank cipher? What would cause an artist open-handedly to enshrine formica, this most artificial and ubiquitous plastic lamination?

Coming of artistic age in the midst of the irreverences of the Pop movement, Artschwager also found resonance in what the mainstream art world had despised. Luxuriating in the fictive swirls of formica, *Diptych #3* takes a degraded medium and makes it art, giving it stature and import in its new incarnation. Artschwager's experiences as a furniture designer and craftsman also are keenly echoed here. He has respect for how objects are structured, and for the pleasure and meaning that can lie in the process of their construction. His considered artisanship opens up possibilities of interpretation at every turn; *Diptych #3* is an object for use—with its use being to question its use. JY

3
Diptych #3, 1967
Formica on wood
68 x 84 x 4 1/2

Richard Artschwager, born Washington, D.C., 1933; lives in Brooklyn, New York

Jo **Baer**

Severe, aloof, impassive, and unyielding, the art of Jo Baer functions as a complete and eloquent realization of the special glories of Minimalism. Works like *Untitled* exemplify many of the concerns that dominated American art in the late 1960s—a feeling of stubbornness and fidelity to a system of thinking, and a determined seriousness that contrasts with some of the amiable and funky excesses of Pop art. Artists such as Baer sought, relished, and achieved the sort of abstract probity that could only be discovered through the application of an almost relentless logic. Everything extraneous was sacrificed as the idea was pared down to its purest essence and presented with near puritanical plainness.

In Baer's case, the causal idea concerned a set of issues about the function and objecthood of painting. Her work is an examination of the actual physical quality of a stretched canvas, its edge, and the reduction of pictorial data to its simplest and least referential voice. These aims are pursued by an inquiry into the fundamental and inherent flatness of painting, the given from which all of Baer's ruminations flow.

Viewers of *Untitled* are asked to pose rather different questions from those that usually occur to us, and to place context over content. Two large canvases are each "framed" by two thin, tasteful painted bands of black and golden brown. All the rest is undifferentiated white, yards and yards of what begins to seem a kind of filler, the pristine interstices between rare events. The paintings are precise replicas of each other, and dominate the wall with willful impenetrability. Baer achieves order, structure, and logic here, eschewing all else in a single-minded pursuit of condensed symmetry.

But in a curious way, what begins to result from her narrowing of information is a sort of dynamic mystery, as if there were a secret, a hidden code lying beneath the surfaces of these paintings. Ultimately, in a way that recalls the massive and silent stone heads that dot Easter Island, these paintings are like sentinels of a forgotten faith, remnants of an agenda that was fully resolved and completed. Shortly after *Untitled* was finished, Baer relocated to Europe. She has subsequently renounced her work as an abstract painter. JY

4
Untitled, 1966-74
Oil on canvas, two panels
each 60 x 84

Jo Baer, born Seattle, 1929;
lives in Amsterdam

form

Kultu

Lothar **Baumgarten**

When Western artists have turned to non-Western cultures, they have tended either to create romantic fantasies about the unspoiled simplicity of "primitive" peoples or to express a conqueror's confidence in the superiority of his own more civilized mode of life. In either case, unquestioned assumptions about racial and cultural hierarchies act as a shield against the transmission of any genuine knowledge of other lives and customs. German artist Lothar Baumgarten attempts to break through that shield. He is interested in revealing the hidden biases of academic disciplines like anthropology, ethnography, and history that investigate the meaning of other cultures. In addition, he suggests how we might get a clearer reading of those on the periphery of our ordinary experience. To these ends, he has created installations in which he inscribes the names of South American Indian tribes, indigenous animals, and tropical plants within the walls of museums and institutions that form the high citadels of European culture. With this transcription, he endeavors to overcome the cultural invisibility of these disappearing worlds.

Baumgarten has also lived for periods of time with the Y̧anomamö Indians of Brazil, adopting their dress, conforming to their customs, and recording their stories. In the artwork he has created from materials collected during these sojourns, he tries to avoid the pitfalls of conventional ethnography: he dispels the illusion of scientific objectivity such field work often projects by acknowledging his own role as observer in photographs of Y̧anomamö activities and settlements. Abandoning the model of cultural purity preferred by traditional anthropologists, Baumgarten incorporates evidence of the clash between the forces of Western encroachment and the tribe's struggle for survival.

He has been particularly concerned with the effects of logging and pollution that threaten to turn the Amazon basin into a wasteland. The photographs from this series suggest the devastation visited on this beautiful region by Western-style development. In his writings, Baumgarten ties the economic exploitation of the landscape to the tradition of colonialism which reduces the value of alien land and peoples to economic utility. In *Kulturform,* as in all his work, the artist encourages us to look beyond our narrow cultural boundaries to a world that is not our own.
EH

5
Kulturform, 1977-85
Three black-and-white photographs,
each 26 1/2 x 33

Lothar Baumgarten, born Rheinsberg, Germany, 1944; lives in Düsseldorf

Bernd and Hilla **Becher**

Proceeding like botanists charting the genealogy of plant species, Bernd and Hilla Becher have embarked on a lifelong project to create a kind of family tree for such generic industrial structures as coal silos, mixing plants, transformers, and, as in this case, water towers. Their investigations have taken them to cities, small towns, and rural areas of Germany, Holland, Belgium, England, France, Luxembourg, and the United States. The data they collect consists of black-and-white documentary photographs of these often peculiar edifices, whose images they then group according to visual and structural similarities. The results take the form seen here, chartlike arrangements of photographs which map the recurrence of basic types across far-flung geographic areas.

While this approach may seem coolly analytic, the final images are surprisingly seductive. The Bechers refer to their finds as "anonymous sculpture," and indeed the simple compromises unknown designers have made between function and ornament in these structures have produced forms of considerable visual interest. Coiling pipes cling like winding tendrils to steel walls, massive tanks rest like sagging bellies on spindly legs, curiously anomalous decorative details—Romanesque arches or Tudor paneling, for instance—overlay otherwise functional designs, suggesting the builders' desire to "beautify" these otherwise prosaic artifacts. The Bechers note that they have discovered certain regional variations—a tendency toward cold functionalism in England, for example, as opposed to a Continental predilection for fantasy and symbolism. As one contemplates the specific details in these arrangements, distinctions between the organic and the industrial begin to blur, and the viewer begins to sense the presence of some kind of evolutionary principle behind their forms.

In their travels, the Bechers avoid the gleaming achievements of high technology. Instead they focus on structures that are old-fashioned, even outmoded. These towers and silos seem to belong to an earlier state of industrial development, like architectural species on the brink of extinction. As a result, an aura of melancholy pervades these images, and we realize that the Bechers are not so much involved simply in collecting and collating data as they are in preserving a record of an industrial landscape soon to be lost forever. Beneath the scientific veneer of the Bechers' project runs a deep strain of romanticism. These structures stand before us with the proud resignation of relics of an industrial past which is already little more than a memory. EH

6
Watertowers (typology), 1980
Nine black-and-white photographs
each 20 x 16

Bernd Becher, born Siegen, Germany, 1931; lives in Düsseldorf;
Hilla Becher, born Potsdam, Germany, 1934; lives in Düsseldorf

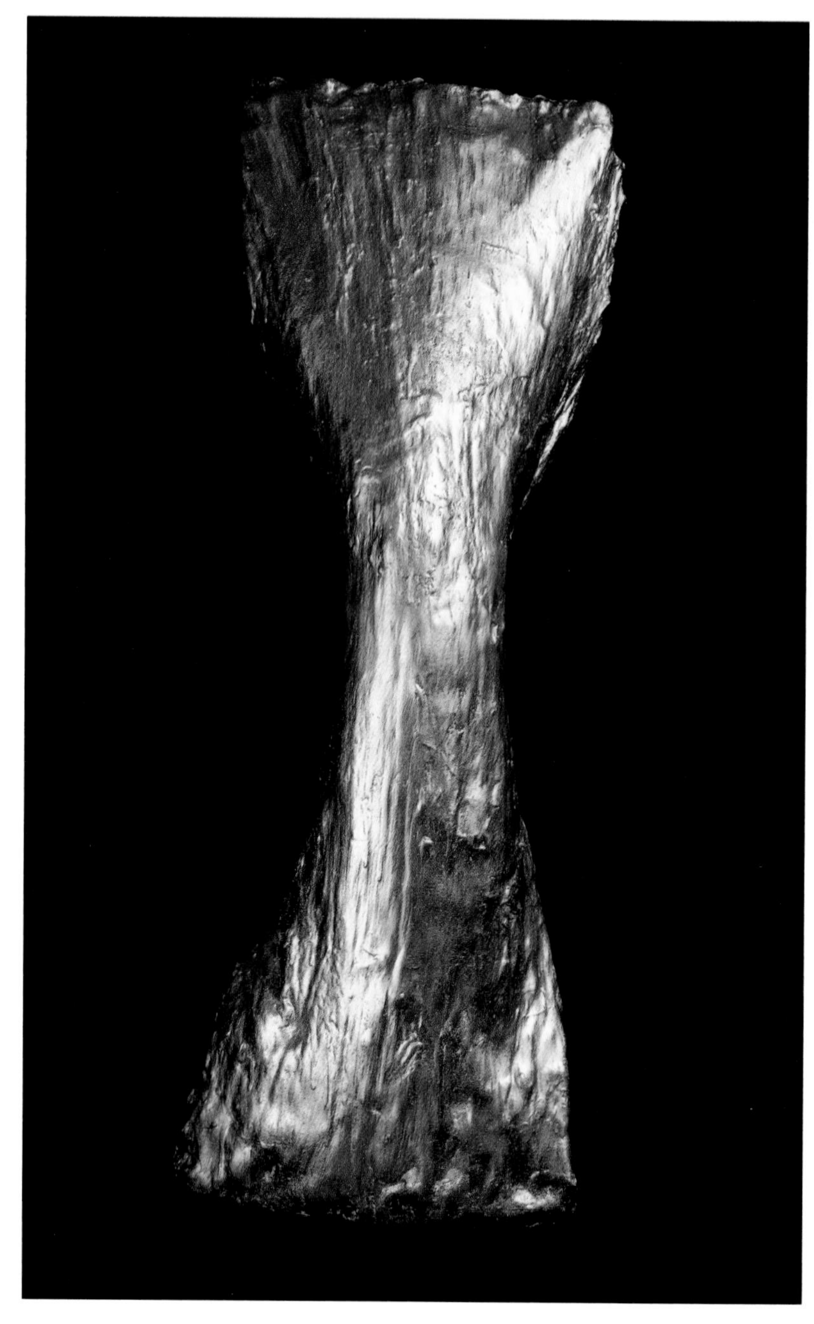

Lynda **Benglis**

Lynda Benglis's art has always been marked by its luxurious and often sensuous immersions into the tactility of materials. In the late 1960s, her paintings composed by pouring pigmented latex rubber directly on the floor caused a reconsideration of what paint and color could mean without the mediating trappings of canvas or wall. These stilled but resonant pools were followed in the 1970s by a bold sequence of wall sculptures, with Benglis challenging the then rather sleepy traditions of modern sculpture. She created stunning and explosive arabesques out of substances as diverse and unexpected as beeswax, cotton bunting, plaster, aluminum screen, and chicken wire. Along with a group of artists collectively known as Postminimalists, Benglis was intrigued with the balance she could strike between her own physical intervention as an artist and the inherent physical possibilities of her materials.

That balance is particularly well achieved in *Spindle*, a swelling gesture of loving excrescence, a fillip of seductive glory. On an armature of chicken wire, Benglis built up a surface of cotton soaked with plaster, and covered that with a layer of gesso. Over this comes the deluge: a rich layering of pure gold leaf turns the rugged and kneaded surface of *Spindle* into a paean of lustrous excess. The sculpture gleams and glitters like untold treasure, a thing of assured value made of the single material we know means wealth and power. It holds its place on the wall with an almost insouciant regal quality, a tightly wrapped statement carrying an aura of authority and prestige.

Although not as specifically as many of her other works, *Spindle* still reflects the feminist concerns that have long been of interest to this artist. The title of the sculpture is culled from the realm of fiber and cloth working, an arena of activity long neglected and denigrated as a "minor art" associated with the world of women. *Spindle* does look like a vertical bow or a bolt of fabric, but here totally transported out of the world of fashion and into that of high art. Its vaguely hourglass, female-torso shape is presented not for its sexual charge, but as a silhouette of honor, striding forward with boldness and presence. In a most interesting way, our sculpture operates like some latter-day Winged Victory of Samothrace, sailing out to us with command and resonance. JY

7
Spindle, 1977
Chicken wire, cotton, plaster, gesso, gold leaf
35 1/2 x 13 1/2 x 6 1/2

Lynda Benglis, born Lake Charles, Louisiana, 1941; lives in New York City

Barbara **Bloom**

Salvador Dali used to note about his work that the success of its flights of surreal fancy depended on his scrupulous realist technique. To undermine reality he had to mimic its own qualities, so as to subvert it from within. There is something of this in Barbara Bloom's *Works for the Blind*, which employs a fury of rationalism and order in order to undercut them, to defuse them and expose their inefficiency and ambiguities. What *are* viewing, seeing, reading, learning, and knowing, and how can our assumptions about these activities be probed?

In this series, Bloom employs the same design principle in all but one piece. Grainy reproductions of photographs depicting events from the world of parapsychology and the paranormal are placed above tiny texts (the letters are approximately 1/16 inch high) printed white on black. Between photo and caption, and overlapping the surface of the former, the text is repeated—in the raised type of braille. Texts and images rarely involve the same subject, at least in a direct sense.

The photograph, one form of "reality," remains readily available to the viewer, but this is like a dream of reality: Bloom's photographs do not adhere to our understanding of what we thought was a rational world. Images of telekinesis, telepathy, mysticism, and UFO's can be read, but only to be doubted and questioned. Is the image truth? Whose truth? Deciphering the Lilliputian texts, moreover, is difficult and ungainly, and can leave one with an annoying sense of being manipulated, particularly when the captions appear arbitrary and concerned with seemingly tepid aphorisms and tracts. Is the word truth? What truth? And yet another language, available only to the sightless and to the few sighted people who read braille, repeats these texts. Bloom cuts openings in the Plexiglas over these pieces to make them accessible by touch, the sense the blind use to see. How do we see? What do we see?

This is like a dream of art, an elusive poetry. A world order of image and word, an understanding of how communication works, and our role as consumers/viewers of art are all critiqued and denied. Bloom takes from us a constant, and leaves us a query, a sweet enigma that kindly and dizzyingly interrogates our suppositions, seeming to promise that a great liberation might follow our unconditional surrender. Question the constant. Layer by layer, something is being exposed; but watch the magician's hands. JY

8
Works for the Blind,
1985-89
Seven offset photographs, braille, photographic text, gold leaf, Plexiglas, metal frames, ed.15
each 32 x 24
(detail)

Barbara Bloom, born Los Angeles, 1951; lives in New York City

Christian **Boltanski**

One of the first facts often noted about Christian Boltanski is his birth in Paris on 6 September 1944, the day of the city's liberation by the Allied armies. That coincidence is emphasized for more than just the sake of biographical curiosity: born at the end of a traumatic period, at the precise moment when postwar France came into being, Boltanski seems particularly well situated to make an inquiry into his nation's legacy. Indeed, his work has always shown a sensitivity to history, but not in geopolitical terms chronicling the rise and fall of nations. Boltanski has instead focused on intimations of individual human dramas, presenting us with poetic evocations of the men and women who in their aggregate comprise history. Works such as *Monument,* from an ongoing series the artist began in 1985, suggest that abstract concepts of history can be particularized in the faces of its survivors and its casualties. He makes us feel as if crucial passages in life, or even events on the order of systematized atrocities, can only be understood by confronting single victims face to face.

The three children who gaze at us from their votive-like altars in *Monument* may or may not have since lost anything more than the innocence of youth and the myriad possibilities open to adolescents at the brink of adulthood. Boltanski does not research what became of them, and in other works has used photos from sources as varied as class pictures from a Jewish School in Vienna in 1931 (inviting speculation on the subjects' subsequent history), and the sixty-two members of the French Mickey Mouse Club in 1955. He grasps the psychological power of religious display and our ingrained respect for this manner of presentation. Setting these teenagers atop pyramids of photos of wrapping paper and crowning the assemblage with the dim illumination of small light bulbs makes them the focus of a shrine. Whatever our religious background, we all understand the fragile and ephemeral quality of youth, and Boltanski asks us to confront its inevitable forfeiture. Like the missing faces that stare at us from milk cartons and bus posters, the three teens here remind us how often our young can be abused and denied fruition. At the heart of *Monument* is a sense of memorial, of lighting a candle to the loss of innocence that either death or maturity must bring. JY

9
Monument, 1988
Photographs, metal frames, electric lights
77 x 91 overall

Christian Boltanski, born Paris, 1944; lives in Paris

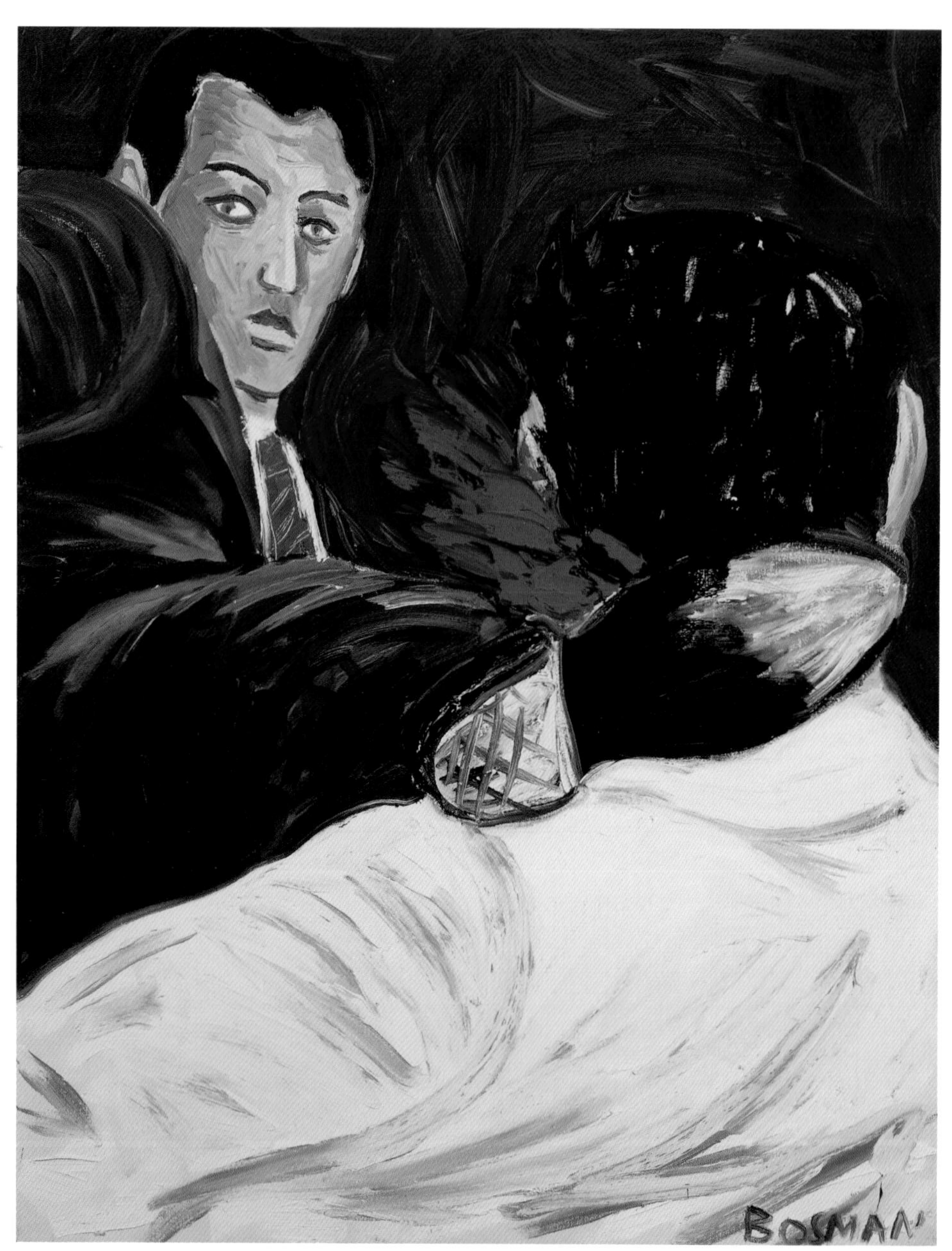
BOSMAN

Richard **Bosman**

Crunch! Oomph! Splat! There's more than cartoon violence at the core of Richard Bosman's paintings, but that isn't a bad place to begin analyzing the work of this most interesting neo-expressionist artist. As in the world of comics, things are pretty clearly defined in Bosman's universe—heroes and villains are tightly limned, and act in accordance with their deepest nature; their actions are unambiguous and direct, with cause and effect closely linked. In paintings like *The Kick,* the kung-fu blows raining onto the side of an opponent's head are always fully deserved, and crisply executed for maximum impact. Blood flows freely, life seems cheap, emotions are heightened, and actions explode with dramatic intensity.

And yet there is a release for us from the intensities of Bosman's world: it lies in our almost instant realization that the narratives played out in his pictures are ultimately dismissible as fiction. *The Kick* functions like a movie poster, a melodramatic promo enticing our vicarious submersion into the cinematic world of the hard-boiled detective. The crunching blow delivered by our handsome hero is his proof of manhood, his labor of Hercules, his test essayed and surpassed. And it thrills, despite our tacit understanding of the principles of suspension of disbelief. This is an episode from a parable world, and blood here is no more, never was any more, than viscous red paint.

Bosman's personal experiences may have led him to be particularly attuned to this charged and mythic presentation of the modern (anti)hero. He was born in India, reared in Indonesia and Egypt, and educated in Australia and England before his arrival in the United States in 1969. Across the globe he watched TV and movies, and read novels and comics, culling the rich fantasy of tough-guy film noir that would eventually form the heart of his subject matter. Part of the onslaught of expressive figuration so characteristic of painting in the early 1980s, *The Kick* successfully exploits its medium; Bosman's slashing and seemingly impatient handling of his brush adds to the impact of his imagery. The painting feels urgent and hurried, the turbulent activity of its surface in harmony with its expressive content. Since that content is finally artificial, a tongue-in-cheek exercise in fiction rather than an aspiration to some more "genuine" truth, Bosman's image and his attitude to it has no air of sincerity, but is steeped in the distancing and cynical atmosphere of irony. JY

10
The Kick, 1981-82
Oil on canvas
62 x 54

Richard Bosman, born Madras, India, 1944; lives in New York City

COPIE

PEINT

ECRIT

Marcel **Broodthaers**

Marcel Duchamp defined the terms of a debate still raging in contemporary art when he distinguished what he called "retinal art" from his own art of ideas. Opposing an art that appeals primarily to the senses and emotions against one that speaks to the mind by means of abstract ideas and philosophical categories, Duchamp laid the groundwork for Conceptual art. A movement that flourished during the 1970s, Conceptual art directed viewers' attention to such issues as the interactions between visual and verbal thinking, the syntax and vocabulary underlying the "language" of visual art, and the relationship between art and "reality," however the latter might be defined. One of the most original and provocative of Duchamp's heirs in this mode was Marcel Broodthaers, a French poet turned artist whose enigmatic drawings, collages, assemblages, and sculptures tease the mind with their attempts to overturn established modes of thought. Broodthaers, who died in 1976, produced a diverse body of work held together, not by some discernible style, but by the evidence it offers of a questing, challenging intellect which could not let the obvious go unexamined.

A recurring theme in Broodthaers' work is the tricky interaction between linguistic and pictorial languages as they strive to represent reality. This three-part work examines that territory. Each drawing contains a splash of red paint accompanied by a single French word. *Peint* (paint) offers a straightforward description of the splash, representing the "normal" relationship between word and image. *Ecrit* (writing), however, offers a more complex interaction. Here the word refers, not to the accompanying image, but to its own function, creating a kind of closed circle which disregards its larger context. Finally, *copie* (copy) suggests that we are to read the paint splash here as a facsimile of the other two. Thus, meaning resides outside the drawing itself and can only be understood in relation to the other elements in the series. With these three drawings, then, Broodthaers suggests the slippery nature of the simple act of reading, demonstrating that a word's sense or signification may dwell in a variety of very different locations.

For Broodthaers, as for many artists who emerged in the seventies, the study of the mechanics of language was an important area of exploration, because it offered evidence of the ways language controls our perception of reality. By exposing inconsistencies in those mechanics, he hoped to undermine that control and open up new areas of freedom for human thought. EH

11
Copie Peint Ecrit,
1972-73
Printing ink, watercolor on paper; three sheets:
11 3/4 x 17 1/2,
11 3/4 x 16 1/4, 14 1/2 x 14

Marcel Broodthaers,
born Brussels, 1924; died in Cologne, 1976

FRIEZE

SITUATED WORK 1987
PAINT ON / UNDER PLEXIGLASS

DANIEL BUREN

CADMIUM GREEN-YELLOW

CADMIUM GREEN MEDIUM

CADMIUM ORANGE LIGHT

CADMIUM ORANGE MEDIUM

CADMIUM RED LIGHT

CADMIUM YELLOW LIGHT

CADMIUM YELLOW MEDIUM

COBALT BLUE

PERMANENT BLACK

PERMANENT GREEN LIGHT

PERMANENT LILAC

PERMANENT ROSE LIGHT

TURQUOISE BLUE

IRIDESCENT GOLD

IRIDESCENT SILVER

Daniel **Buren**

12
Frieze, Situated Work,
1987
Acrylic, Plexiglas, 132 sheets, each 36 x 36, installed 99 x 2232 x 636 overall

Daniel Buren, born Bouligne-Billancourt, France, 1938; lives in Paris

Since 1967, Daniel Buren has been working *in situ*, that is, in direct response to a given location or situation. Perhaps the first artist to adopt this Latin phrase to describe his on-site commissions, Buren associates it with all his works, which he executes in museums, galleries, private collections, or public spaces. Initially desiring to strip painting of illusionistic reference or expressive characteristics, so that it might function purely as a sign of itself, Buren had decided in 1965 to reduce the pictorial content of his work to the repetition of alternating white and colored vertical bands about 3 1/2 inches wide. He realized, moreover, that he did not have to paint these bands himself, but could purchase canvas used for awnings or outdoor furniture, or order printed material to suit his particular needs.

Such commercially obtained, prefabricated material with its vertical stripes–intended to be as neutral a (de)sign as possible–serves Buren in an aesthetic practice that frees the work from the framing edge of the canvas. He has directed his concerns away from the canvas field as an area of exclusive activity to examine and expose the work of art's affiliation with its surroundings. The specific placement of striped material thus governs the form and meaning of the work and in each instance allows Buren to explore and visually highlight its contextual frame of reference.

Buren's Refco installation encircles the New York Trading Room like an architectural frieze, punctuated by variations in the ceiling and by columns and windows. The various colors–twelve in all plus black–proceed symmetrically in alphabetical order from two axes and serve to unify the encompassing enclosure. Unlike most works of art, Buren's installation may be seen from anywhere in the room, yet can never be viewed as a whole from a single vantage point. Furthermore, mirrored stripes draw the reality of the cityscape into the reality of the interior. In this way, the existing environment participates in the work's visual content. Art and nature thereby converge in a work that also structurally reflects itself. Offering a panoply of colors that mirror each other while embracing the architectural framework of the room, *Frieze, Situated Work* also incorporates the real world outside the windows–and supersedes the traditional boundaries of painting. AR

John **Cage**

13
(2R)/9 (Where R=Ryoanji), 1983
Pencil on paper
10 x 19

(4R)/4 (Where R=Ryoanji), 1983
Pencil on paper
10 x 19

(13R)/14 (Where R=Ryoanji), 1983
Pencil on paper
10 x 19

(3R)/7 (Where R=Ryoanji), 1983
Pencil on paper
10 x 19
(Clockwise, from top left)

John Cage, born Los Angeles, 1912; lives in New York City

Foremost among John Cage's aesthetic concerns has been a consistent endeavor to blur distinctions between art and life, to remove the inevitable impediments modern existence places between them. His life's work—most often as a composer of avant-garde music, but also as a visual artist—has been an effort to touch and reveal essences, and to strive for a kind of purity that is transcendent in nature. Cage has steadfastly walked the risky line separating chance from chaos, examining the murky areas that lie between the possible poetry of randomness and its antithesis in meaninglessness.

Since the 1930s, much of Cage's reputation lies in his activities in the world of music. Compositions like *4' 33"* (1952), a silent piece in three movements, or *Music for Piano* (1955), which took all of its notes from stains and imperfections in his music paper, show Cage's obsession with chance and randomness. Harmony for Cage often rests in achieving a state of receptivity wherein one's senses are acutely heightened toward the understanding, recognition, and revelation of some discrete phenomenon. A lifelong interest in and commitment to Buddhism and Oriental culture have enhanced Cage's attempts to render invisible the gap between the simple and the complex.

These attempts have extended beyond the realm of musical composition. Since 1942, Cage has been collaborating with dancer/choreographer Merce Cunningham on a series of ongoing projects, and his interaction in the 1950s with artists such as Marcel Duchamp, Robert Rauschenberg, and Jasper Johns is well known. Although Cage had painted since the 1930s, it was in the late 1960s that he began more regularly to incorporate art making into his life.

In his Ryoanji series, Cage creates metaphysical equivalences for the famous Ryoanji rock gardens in Kyoto, Japan. His cryptic titles actually function as equations of his activities. Ryoanji is made up of five groups of fifteen rocks; Cage took fifteen stones from his own rock collection, arranged them by chance according to the *I Ching*, and traced their outlines as many times as each title indicates, multiplied by R, which is fifteen. The equation (4R)/4 means that sixty tracings occur on the paper, using four different pencils. Cage's effort is a discovery of poetry, an act of grace; his delicate line describes both a place and an attitude, and wends its way across the paper's surface, heading for nirvana. JY

John **Chamberlain**

Although he has worked with many other materials, John Chamberlain remains most closely associated with his "signature" substance—crushed automobile parts. In his work, crumpled fenders, doors, and other sections of old car bodies are woven together in complex abstract sculptures whose colors come from a palette determined by the whims of Detroit. There is a certain shock in seeing America's number-one consumer item treated so irreverently, but Chamberlain insists that he is not really interested in car parts per se—they are simply a source of available material, much as marble was to sculptors in Michelangelo's day. In fact, despite the novelty of Chamberlain's material, his work addresses the same sculptural issues that concerned many of his contemporaries.

As a young man during the 1950s, Chamberlain immersed himself in New York's exciting downtown art scene. Sharing with young artists like Robert Rauschenberg and Jasper Johns an impatience with conventional materials and techniques, he also sympathized with the older abstract expressionist painters in his circle, for whom art was a matter of spontaneity and the direct expression of feeling. Thus, Chamberlain rejected the time-consuming labor associated with traditional sculpture. His early work is strongly influenced by David Smith, whose primitivistic steel and aluminum sculptures were welded from separate parts rather than cast in one piece. With his discovery of the expressive potential of car parts, however, Chamberlain began to abandon the more overt figural or totemic references in his mentor's work in favor of a mode that some have termed, because of its sense of motion and gesture, abstract expressionist sculpture.

A Chamberlain sculpture is almost always self-supporting—the various pieces are nestled in an organic whole and only later welded together for ease in transportation. In his earlier work, the artist almost never added to the crumpled metal's given color. Since 1974, however, he has begun to make his own additions, reworking the lacquered surfaces of the body parts before assembly and even at times spraying a streak of color over the newly completed sculpture. Although formed of crushed steel, Chamberlain's sculptures convey an impression less of violence than of a malleable fleshiness, creating an odd marriage of the industrial and the organic. In the end, they transcend their prosaic origins to become rich and visually rewarding examples of abstract sculpture. EH

14
Sabine Knights, 1977
Painted and chromium-plated steel
74 x 30 1/2 x 10 1/2

John Chamberlain, born Rochester, Indiana, 1927; lives in Sarasota, Florida

Surrounded Islands (project for Biscayne Bay, Greater Miami, Florida) Venetian Causeway, J. Tuttle Causeway, 79 th. str. Causeway, Broad Causeway
Christo 1983
Woven polypropylene Fabric (Gr 0.48) covering the surface of the water, extending into the Bay
Island #11 width 150 - 200 Feet
200 Feet length 1025 FT.
anchor and Boom 6.3 FT.
the Floating Fabric attached to a long Boom (in sections of 100 Feet, diameter 12" Reinforced)

Christo

One of the most important aspects of Christo's environmental mega-projects since the 1960s has been their ephemeral nature. It is crucial to the artist that these extraordinary events be brief and fleeting, that enormous effort and expense be put to occurrences that are transitory, until his pieces take on something of the air of a happening or a performance. In 1969, for instance, Christo wrapped one million square feet of Australia's coastline with erosion-control mesh, for ten weeks. For his 1972 *Valley Curtain,* he used 200,000 square feet of orange nylon to block a valley in Colorado, for only twenty-eight hours. Four years later, *Running Fence* ran an eighteen-foot high barrier of white nylon fabric twenty-four miles across two California counties, for fourteen days. The spectacular *Surrounded Islands Project* of 1983 involved eleven small islands in Florida's Biscayne Bay, each surrounded by a total of 6.5 million square feet of pink woven polypropylene fabric, for two weeks.

Each of these colossal projects and others required months, often years, of intense planning and negotiation, and the cooperation of hundreds of assistants and volunteers. *Surrounded Islands* was more than two years in organizing, and Christo needed the continual and costly support of lawyers, marine biologists, ornithologists, mammal experts, marine engineers, and builder-contractors, in addition to the use of a blimp hangar and a work force of 430. His concept was discussed in several dozen public hearings, and he had to secure permits from eight separate governmental agencies, including the U.S. Army Corps of Engineers and the Dade County Department of Environmental Resources Management. But all this was not an impediment to Christo; he has always seen the maelstrom of logistics, collaboration, and public activity he endures to execute his projects as part of what gives them their meaning, as what turns them from one individual's idea into a communal event.

This drawing and altered photograph served several purposes for Christo. It was one more document of his planning, and a resource to help raise part of the millions of dollars *Surrounded Islands* cost to realize. Like a fragment of the Berlin Wall, it is a souvenir, a piece of evidence—in this case anticipatory—of a thing that exists now most fully only in memory. In the truest sense, it is the practical means to a stupendous end. JY

15
Surrounded Islands Project for Biscayne Bay, 1983
Pastel, charcoal, pencil, crayon, enamel paint, aerial photograph; two parts
42 1/2 x 65 1/2,
15 1/2 x 65 1/2

Christo, born Gabrovo, Bulgaria, 1935; lives in New York City

Tony **Cragg**

A romanticized vision of nature has been a mainstay of British art since the nineteenth century, from the idealized landscape paintings of John Constable and J. M. W. Turner to the remote nature walks of contemporary artist Richard Long. The work of Tony Cragg, like that of other representatives of the so-called New British Sculpture, flies in the face of that tradition. Cragg finds both his materials and his content in the ephemeral discards of urban civilization, creating sculptures that speak with dark humor about the downside of modern industrial progress. Many of his works take the form of collages of rubbish he has collected from city streets and trash heaps. He has frequently gathered bits of brightly colored plastic debris—scraps of plastic buckets, toy guns, kitchen utensils, and detergent bottles—assembling them into simple and immediately readable silhouettes of figures, crescent moons, or the Union Jack. These works provide an odd interplay between the still recognizable building blocks of which they are made and the larger image they form together.

In *Dining Motions,* Cragg offers a variation on that technique. A fractured image of knife, fork, spoon, and bisected sausage emerges disjointedly from a broken surface composed of pieces of painted wood arranged on the wall like a jigsaw puzzle. A close look reveals that the wood has been culled from a variety of sources. Some pieces are evidently scraps of plywood left over from construction projects; others once formed sections of cabinets or tables; one is a complete door. The pieced-together composition vaguely suggests the mosaic technique used in ancient and medieval palaces and churches. However, such highbrow references are immediately undercut both by the banality of the image, which refers to dining as it is practiced at the lower end of the social spectrum, and by the prosaic sources of the wood pieces themselves.

Cragg's choice of materials that exhibit traces of their former lives allows his sculpture to point beyond the art world back into everyday reality. Thus his works form a quiet attack on the precious status art generally assumes in contemporary culture. Instead of extending a fantasy of harmony and beauty, they turn the English landscape tradition on its head, celebrating, not the cultivated nature of field and garden, but the gritty manmade environment of the city. EH

16
Dining Motions, 1988
Mixed media
100 x 200 overall

Tony Cragg, born Liverpool, 1949; lives in Wuppertal, West Germany

Carroll **Dunham**

17
Green + Yellow, 1986
Mixed media on elm veneer
29 3/4 x 24

Carroll Dunham, born New Haven, Connecticut, 1949; lives in New York City

If one strain of twentieth-century abstraction has tended toward an ideal of purity and calm, another is characterized by almost manic intensity. The latter often manifests itself in canvases that teem with biomorphic shapes, dividing and metamorphosing like microscopic organisms in some biologist's petri dish. The work of Carroll Dunham is firmly lodged within this tradition. His paintings suggest abstract explosions and are full of cartoony organic forms, captured as if on the brink of mutation. Many of these forms make reference to the human body: we can make out elements that suggest fragmented body parts, sexual organs, or bodily secretions. Other shapes bring to mind single-celled organisms multiplying before our eyes.

Dunham's approach recalls automatic drawing, a technique practiced by the Surrealists as a means of countering the constraints of the rational mind. Adopting the model of free association from psychoanalysis, surrealist artists let chance determine their compositions, sometimes drawing with eyes closed, searching for compositions in random scribbles, or passing the same drawing from artist to artist. During the early 1940s, surrealist-influenced painters like Jackson Pollock and Arshile Gorky also experimented with such activities, which they hoped would bring them closer to a kind of dream state where the unconscious might speak more directly. Dunham seeks a similar freedom, often painting over a wood veneer surface, allowing the meandering grain and knots to become the first layer of his composition. Working in collaboration with this pre-existing pattern, he allows the whorls and lines in the wood to suggest forms or act as counterpoint to the images he has invented.

But if Dunham extends a tradition, he is also very much an artist of his own time. Coming of age in the early 1980s, he has created work that exudes the air of playful rebellion then dominant in the art world. Like his contemporaries Jean-Michel Basquiat, Keith Haring, and Kenny Scharf, Dunham has been fascinated by sources such as graffiti, Saturday morning cartoons, and bathroom humor, which challenge the canons of good taste surrounding "high art." Thus, although these drawings and paintings have an impressive historical pedigree, the final effect of Dunham's exuberant compositions is anything but stodgy. Irreverent and brash, they celebrate the flux of the prerational mind while encouraging us to find a kind of poetry in the background noise of urban life. EH

MIRACLE

Nancy **Dwyer**

Words as we normally experience them, strung together in sentences or spread neatly across the pages of newspapers and books, are transparent things which dissolve in the presence of the meanings they are intended to convey. In Nancy Dwyer's paintings and sculptures, however, words themselves become a focus of interest. She may sculpt a single word, such as "stay" or "envy," out of furniture-sized blocks of granite or marble, so that their blocky letters confront the viewer like a set of eccentrically shaped tombstones. Or, she may make a single word or simple phrase the subject of a painting, imbuing it with importance and monumentality by embellishing it in the style of television advertising.

In either case, the word becomes a thing in its own right, exuding a physical presence. By isolating individual words and phrases in this way, Dwyer is able to undermine their normal functions. At times, she turns them into visual puns by playing texture or material off against the word's actual meaning. In other cases, she introduces subtle discrepancies which point to the abuses and distortions of language that occur in a media-inundated society.

Miracle demonstrates this approach. Inscribed in an arching gold arrow, the word "MIRACLE" soars through the air like a shooting star. Its style and format are familiar, recalling that of corporate logos or brand names. In the presence of this compelling word-image, we almost forget that the conventional definition of the word refers to supernatural phenomena rather than the properties of dish soap or laundry detergent. As is often the case in the world of advertising and product marketing, superlatives are overused and claims are so exaggerated that their common meanings are lost. The image thus becomes a monument to the ability of hype to remake ordinary language.

Dwyer has deliberately rejected the esoteric visual language of "high art" for the flashy glitz of mass media, reminding us at once of advertising's seductiveness and its dangers. Her embrace of popular culture may seem problematic to keepers of the flame of high art, but, as she recently told curator Marcia Tucker in *Artforum,* "the biggest art issue is learning about being in the world." EH

18
Miracle, 1987
Acrylic on canvas,
two parts
60 x 75 overall

Nancy Dwyer, born
New York City, 1954;
lives in New York City

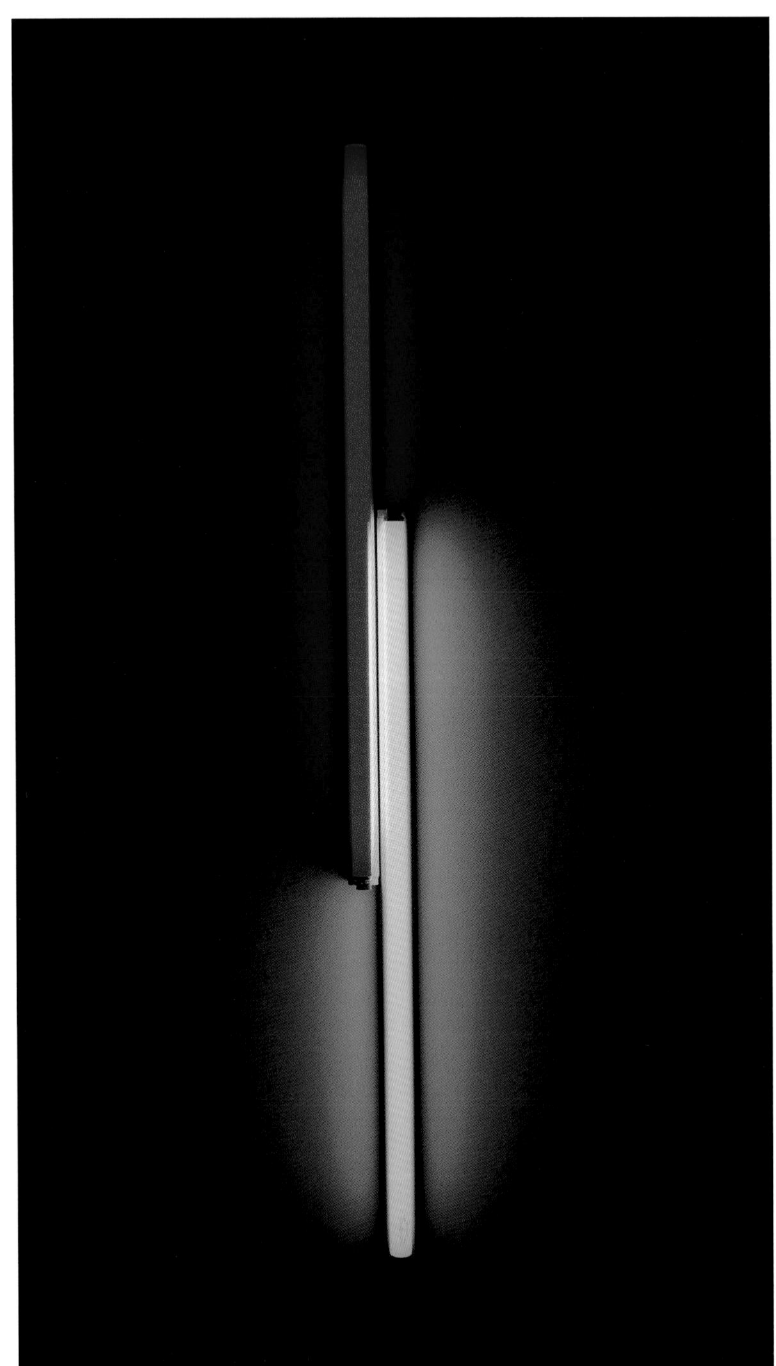

Dan **Flavin**

19
Untitled, 1968
Two fluorescent tubes
72 x 5 x 4

Dan Flavin, born New York City, 1933; lives in Wainscott, New York

Abstract and pristine, Dan Flavin's *Untitled* sculpture exploits technological possibilities to create an art environment. Its flood of fluorescent light extends its reality outside of its own boundaries: it actively enters our world, subtly assaulting us as we approach and leave it, illuminating our space, casting a glow we cannot ignore, and altering any context in which it is displayed. It *is* sculpture, but not of the customary inert elements of stone or metal or glass or clay; rather, *Untitled* is electrically constituted light, itself one of the miracles of the modern world, here bent to new purposes of illumination.

Flavin has been using light as a medium for sculpture for almost twenty-five years, first inspired by the illuminated corridors of the Museum of Natural History in New York, where he worked as a guard. He was intrigued by the possibilities of drama and energy inherent in light itself, in its ability to sustain interest and evoke a curious and mysterious kind of presence. His subsequent inquiries have been ruminations on that presence, and, whether as large as forty-three feet and made up of dozens of elements, or as modest and circumspect as Refco's *Untitled*, Flavin's sculptures and installations ask us to rethink the parameters of art. Composed of energy, of elements that deny or modify their own form, Flavin's sculptures border on dematerialization; they are contourless, open, and mutable.

Untitled is comprised of two fluorescent tubes, one red, one green, each four feet in length, and set side by side vertically to overlap for precisely two feet. In a way, the piece possesses the silhouette of an abstract assemblage, a pair of colored stripes given a new dimension through electricity. Each color shines in a luminous aura, enveloping its environs in pools of radiant light. This red and green glow—Flavin, parenthetically, has rarely used these colors together—merges in areas to form an unpleasant and acidic orange tone that has great retinal impact, that seems to hum forth, calling for our attention. We, as Flavin intends, become the arena on which the artwork is played out, our response to this intrusive wall-sculpture taking center stage as our consciousness of ourselves as observers and participants is splendidly heightened.   JY

Günther **Förg**

20
Untitled (Newport), 1988
Acrylic on wood, twelve panels each 25 3/4 x 19 1/2 (detail)

Günther Förg, born Fussen, West Germany, 1952; lives in Areuse, Switzerland

For a viewer versed in its conventions, the abstract art of the twentieth century is a kind of visual language. Forms and colors can be arranged to express emotional states or their absence, can embody a rage for order or the seductions of chaos. On superficial acquaintance, the work of German artist Günther Förg seems to partake of that language. A closer look, however, reveals that he has reduced the syntax and grammar of abstraction to a kind of gibberish which may look reassuringly familiar, but which is finally opaque and unreadable.

The paintings in this series, for instance, appear to come out of a tradition of geometric abstraction that runs from Piet Mondrian and Kasimir Malevich early in the century to the later color fields of Mark Rothko and Ad Reinhardt. But it would in fact be a mistake to seek meaning in any one of Förg's paintings by itself. There is an arbitrary quality to the stripes and rectangles almost lackadaisically swathed across their surfaces, and the colors—dirty shades of red, blue, black, and green—are peculiarly inexpressive. Moreover, as these small panels march monotonously across the wall, with a sense of almost military precision, the viewer's attention is deflected away from the individual paintings to the architectural space they occupy.

To understand what Förg is up to, it is important to know that he works in a variety of other modes as well. He creates room-scale installations, large wall reliefs of poured lead, and floor-to-ceiling black-and-white architectural photographs. The latter, which focus on public buildings from the 1920s and thirties, are especially revealing. In these works, Förg focuses on architectural details that enhance the ordered, often oppressive geometry of these structures. In doing so, he reminds us that high Modernism, the period in art and architecture that these buildings represent, was a movement devoted to purity, harmony, and unity, ideals that turned out to be disturbingly compatible with the program of fascism. As a German artist, Förg is particularly sensitive to the implications of such utopian yearnings. Thus, in all his works, there is an undercurrent of criticism directed against Modernism's impossible promises. In this light, it becomes clear that the curious opacity of the paintings in this series is intentional. Förg directs our attention outward, beyond the picture frame to a disjointed and fractured reality, while he warns us that this fragmentation can only be made whole in our most dangerous fantasies. EH

H.R.H. THE DUKE OF EDINBURGH
THINKING ABOUT THE RIVER THAMES
Gilbert + George
1981

Gilbert and George

21
H.R.H. The Duke of Edinburgh Thinking about the River Thames, 1981
Collaged postcards
46 1/4 x 28 3/4

Gilbert, born Dolomites, Italy, 1943; lives in London; George, born Devon, England 1942; lives in London

Mixing politics and aesthetics, the sacred and the profane, "official culture" and images of the dispossessed, Gilbert and George are the provocateurs of contemporary British art. In their school days, the duo decided to subsume their individuality beneath a joint persona and to devote their lives to art. During the 1960s, they went so far as to declare themselves "living sculptures" whose every movement and gesture was a work of art. In their subsequent photo collages, their own images play a prominent role. Dressed contrary to the artist stereotype in conservative business suits, they stand defined by a thick black outline and juxtaposed against iconic images of flowers, crosses, heraldic symbols, or soaring architectural structures.

These works, with their symbolic colors and formally arranged images, resemble medieval stained-glass windows. At the same time, they also offer social commentary, mixing symbols of upper-class conformism and respectability with reminders of the realities of class, chaos, and poverty which society would prefer remained invisible. Yet the art of Gilbert and George is unlike traditional social realism, which is generally designed to incite a sense of moral outrage at the conditions it exposes. These artists affect a studied passivity, appearing in their images primarily as spectators or voyeurs detached from the scenes and events around them. As a result, their attitude toward the phenomena they present is ambiguous.

H.R.H. The Duke of Edinburgh Thinking about the River Thames is from a series of "postcard sculptures," composed of arrangements of the most banal sort of tourist postcards. The images here—a state portrait of the Duke of Edinburgh and a scenic view of the Thames River—clearly offer us an England as she would like to see herself, devoid of turmoil, existing in seamless continuity with tradition, and watched over by a benevolent monarchy. In fact, however, the stiffness of the Duke's pose and the obviously retouched quality of the scenic vistas convey an impression of artifice and suggest the instability of this airbrushed vision of England. The repetition of the postcard images underscores their contrivance, while the work as a whole, in its dry humored way, ironically undermines the conventions it only appears to uphold. EH

CURB YOUR ANIMAL
INSTINCT
CONTROLA
TUS INSTINCTO ANIMALE

Ilona **Granet**

Armed with the recognition that our culture speaks more clearly about its innermost desires and fantasies through the medium of advertising than through art, many contemporary artists have begun to play with the format and style of commercials, billboards, and magazine ads. The work of Ilona Granet, for instance, might at first glance be mistaken for the kind of sprightly advertising and public service messages that dominated the mass media of the 1950s. In her mock signs and billboards, we glimpse again the dutiful company man, the overbearing boss, the primly efficient secretary, the all-competent mom—all those role models designed to complement a postwar era of prosperity and progress. However, Granet resurrects these images not to revive the values they embody, but to expose the dangers they obscure. Thus, in a series of billboards placed near the site of Love Canal, she adopts the bright tone of chamber-of-commerce boosterism, welcoming visitors to a community whose emblems include nuclear reactors and barrels of hazardous waste.

In the series that includes *Curb Your Animal Instinct,* Granet takes on the issue of sexual harassment in the work place. Small signs of the sort that might normally designate a no-smoking area or contain public service announcements here offer admonishments against sexually abusive language or behavior. Using a graphic style reminiscent of the fifties to portray wolf-headed men and their put-upon female employees, Granet carries the caricatures to such extremes that the absurdity and degradation of the rigid sexual roles of that era become apparent. With wit and style, she reminds us that those attitudes are not so remote from the contemporary work place as we might wish to believe.

Granet's decision to deal with pressing contemporary issues in a format that both mimics and mocks the folksy tone of postwar advertising allows her to make a point about the dangers of the kind of complacency that characterized that era. When a citizenry has too much reverence for authority and the better judgment of experts and too little awareness of the darker aspects of human nature, it becomes easy, her mock messages suggest, to sacrifice freedom for order and individual rights for social harmony. Clever and immediately accessible, her admonitions are designed to make us smile and then to make us think. EH

22
Curb Your Animal Instinct, 1987
Silkscreen on metal, ed. 100
24 x 24

Ilona Granet, born Brooklyn, New York, 1948; lives in New York City

Philip **Guston**

23
The Wall II, 1975
Oil on canvas
60 x 88 1/2

Philip Guston, born Montreal, 1913; died in Woodstock, New York, 1981

It is rare for a well-known and successful artist to shift gears radically in his later years. One of the unusual exceptions was Philip Guston, who worked in a social realist mode in his youth before achieving a solid reputation as the creator of lyrical painterly abstractions in the 1950s and sixties. Then in 1968, when Guston was fifty-five, his work changed dramatically. To the shock and dismay of many of his long-time supporters, he began to paint crudely childlike images of bulbous heads and bloodshot eyeballs floating over bleak landscapes, scrambled piles of shoes and bottles and broken watches, and blank-eyed, hooded Klansmen.

Appearing at a moment of great social and political turmoil, these darkly humorous tableaux were as inspiring to younger artists as they were perplexing to the art establishment. Today, following a decade in which emotionally powerful figurative painting has often dominated the art scene, it is hard to imagine the initial impact of these works. With their cartoon style and references to daily life, Guston's late paintings seemed superficially related to Pop art but were in fact far removed from its cool, cerebral tone. Eschewing Pop's focus on icons of consumer culture, Guston internalized his images. Beneath their humor, these quirky paintings express a very personal sense of anger and loss, forming a portrait of the artist as an old and often melancholy man.

The autobiographical aspects of this work are unmistakable. The bare light bulb that appears in many of these paintings refers to the artist's childhood, when he used to withdraw to a closet to draw, while the Klansman and the bulbous head serve as self-mocking alter egos. In *The Wall*, we see a number of vintage Guston symbols. The wall itself, massive and unyielding, evokes a recurring feeling of frustration. The shoes suggest the artist's presence, and conjure as well dreams of escape. Vainly scattered over the landscape, they evoke the wreck of hope, smothered by an old artist's sense of unfulfilled aspiration. Taken together then, these elements, the bottles, and the black insect, offer not so much a concrete narrative as a picture of a state of mind in which absurdity, futility, and humor are inextricably mixed.

Since his death in 1980, Guston has become a hero to many younger artists for whom his powerful imagery and gutsy independence from art-world fashion serve as a model for artistic practice. Refusing to rest on his laurels, Guston, in his later years, pushed deeply into his own heart of darkness, in the process casting a glow on some of the darker corners of human experience. EH

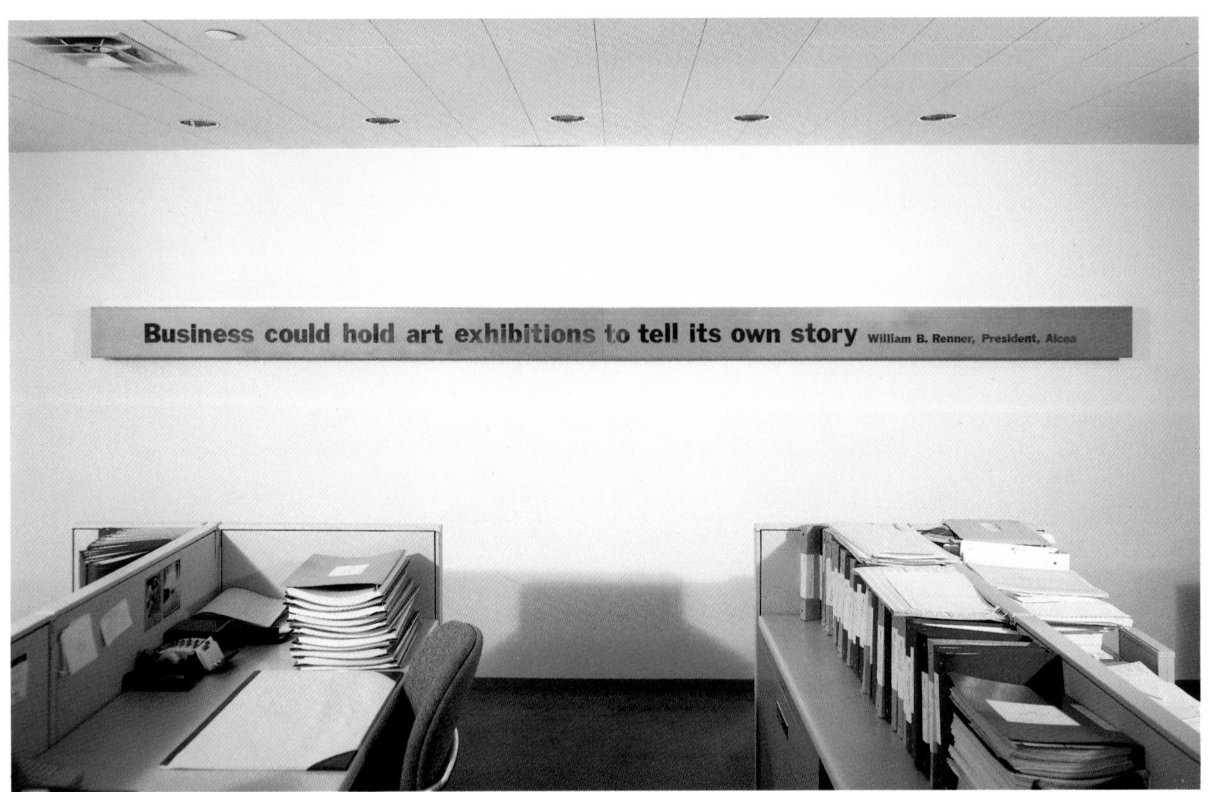
Business could hold art exhibitions to tell its own story William B. Renner, President, Alcoa

Hans **Haacke**

As crisp, pristine, and high-tech as tomorrow's corporate logo, Hans Haacke's longitudinal wall sculpture appropriates a specific cultural language only to undermine it, to expose it for what he feels it may attempt to obscure. Haacke senses real dangers in the world of promotional corporate-speak, and more specifically in the ways corporate America has used art as a public relations tool. His work is a straightforward and sobering call to ethics, an investigation of the somewhat muddy and insidious incentives that might accompany institutional patronage of the visual arts.

In recent decades, the art world and corporate America have indeed become constant bedfellows. In 1967, support given to the arts by American corporations totaled some $22 million; by 1987, that sum grew to almost $1 billion. Corporate sponsorship of museums, exhibitions, and not-for-profit organizations, as well as purchases from galleries and artists have become staple features of the business of art. Philippe de Montebello, Director of the Metropolitan Museum of Art, told the *New York Times* in 1985 that the Met was "dependent on corporate sponsorship."

At what cost? Haacke's art points to two concerns. The first is the possibility that this fiscal patronage may lead to a chilling climate of censorship or control at art institutions that rely on corporate support. Haacke himself was the object of such censorship in a famous incident in 1971, when his exhibition scheduled at the Guggenheim Museum was canceled because he planned a series of photo-and-text panels documenting the slum-housing profits of several specific New York businessmen. This, the museum's board of directors decided, was not art.

Haacke is also sensitive to the ways corporations use their support of the arts as a public relations strategy, buying culture as the ultimate subterfuge. The bravura of Alcoa president William Renner's statement, the clear and pointblank manner in which he views art as an instrument for promotion and aggrandizement seems a confirmation of many of Haacke's fears. The artist presents Renner's assertion without comment, in the trappings of a corporate style in gleaming aluminum, knowing we will see through the slick commercial presentation to the manipulative and sordid motives below. Haacke hopes we will rethink Alcoa's motto, "We can't wait for tomorrow," and that we will recognize the potential abuses residing in such questionable impetuosity. JY

24
Alcoa: We Can't Wait for Tomorrow, 1979
Mirror-polished aluminum letters on square aluminum tubing
9 x 192 x 4 1/2

Hans Haacke, born Cologne, Germany, 1936; lives in New York City

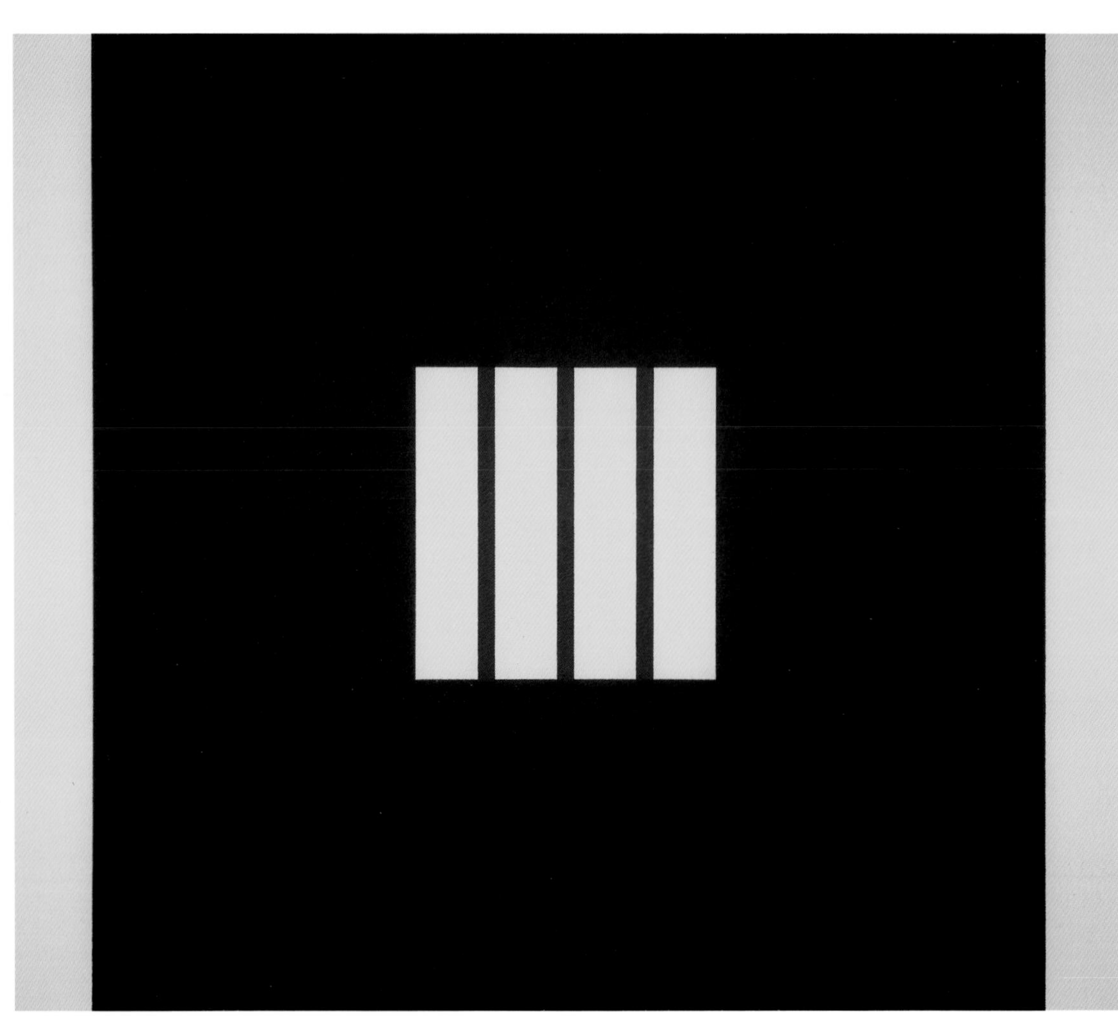

Peter **Halley**

The paintings of Peter Halley, like the abstract panels of Günther Förg, have a familiar look to any one acquainted with the history of twentieth-century art. Halley's simple blocks and bars of color arranged against solid backgrounds bring to mind the measured geometry of Piet Mondrian, the luminous color fields of Barnett Newman, and the grand simplicity of two-color canvases by Ellsworth Kelly. In fact, however, Halley is less interested in continuing the traditions of Constructivism, Minimalism, and color-field painting than in turning them inside out. Along with many artists of his generation (he is in his thirties), Halley is deeply suspicious of the grand claims made on behalf of art earlier in the century. His predecessors enshrined absolutes like purity and truth, abstracting and simplifying their compositions in an effort to get at the "essence" of things. Halley, by contrast, uses geometry as a symbol of alienation.

Like any good revolutionary, he mounts his attack using protective coloration borrowed from his adversaries. Thus, in his hands, elemental forms such as squares and rectangles, which other artists have used to escape the contingencies and contradictions of the workaday world, are models for what Halley calls the "geometricization of modern life." By this he refers to the predicament of the lone individual in a modern urban society, whom he sees as connected to the outside world only through a bewildering array of complex electronic and technological networks involving telephones, televisions, computers, and electrical circuits.

In Halley's world, our normal sense that we can control our lives is an illusion. Instead, each of us is merely a tiny node in a vast geometrical matrix. In order to create a heightened sense of distance from a pre-technological, supposedly more "natural" state of affairs, Halley employs patently artificial colors and materials, favoring Day-glo reds, yellows, and oranges and frequently adding a texture of stucco.

Prison with Yellow Background is one of a series of works in which the artist explores the idea of geometry as an image of confinement. Here he takes the luminous color square employed by earlier modernist painters as a metaphor for the liberation of consciousness and literally places it behind bars. No longer a joyous symbol of the triumph of spirit over matter, geometric abstraction here becomes a sad monument to the false myth of individuality. EH

25
Prison with Yellow Background, 1984
Day-glo paint and Rollo-tex on canvas
60 x 70

Peter Halley, born New York City, 1953; lives in New York City

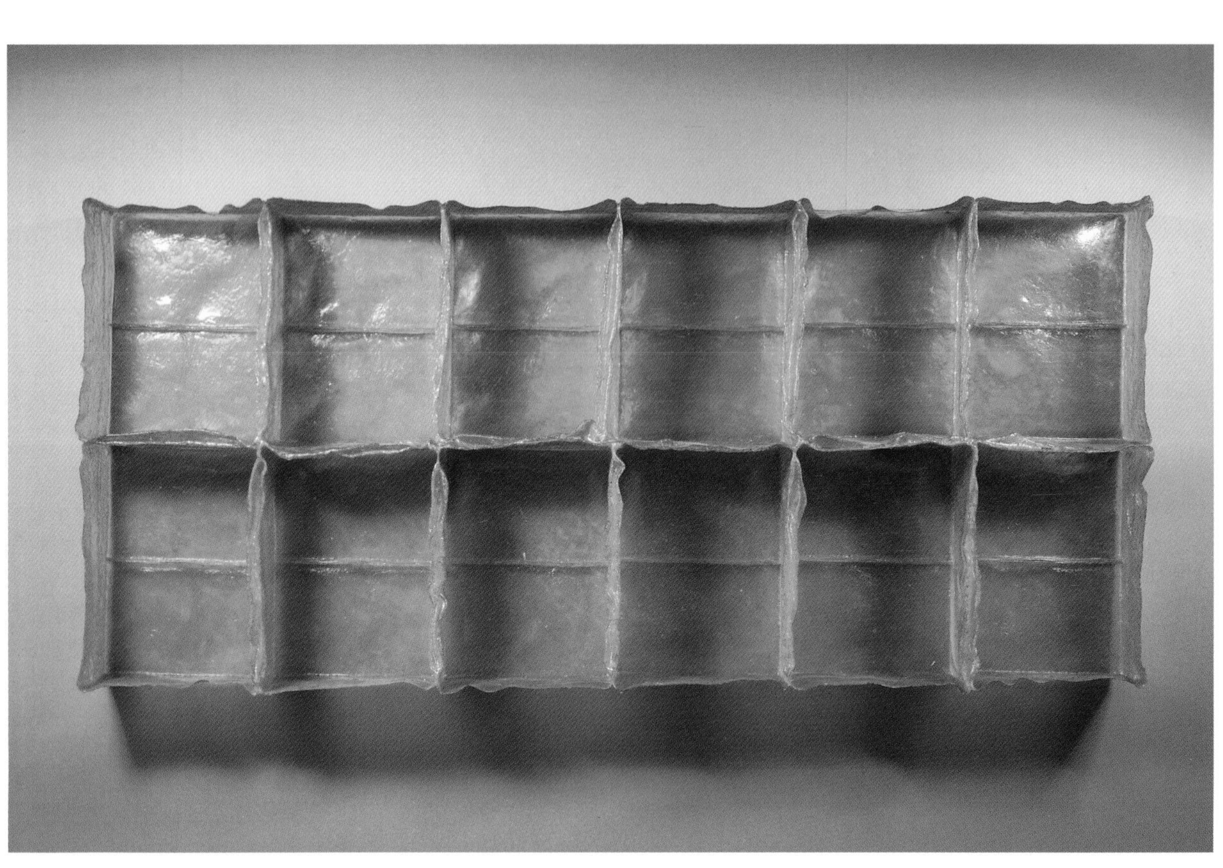

Eva **Hesse**

A sculpture of special historical significance, *Sans II* functions as a legacy from one of the briefest but most interesting careers in modern art. Eva Hesse's tragic death from a brain tumor at the age of thirty-four in 1970 cut short a vision that had already made a deep impact on the art world. By then her work had been collected by institutions such as the Museum of Modern Art and the Whitney Museum of American Art in New York, and she was widely recognized as one of the most talented of a group of artists investigating new and largely malleable sculptural substances. In Hesse's hands, fiberglass, rubberized cheesecloth, rubber tubing, and polyethylene sheets could be made to exude a strong sense of tactility, weight, and presence, while also seeming poignant, vulnerable, and ultimately perishable.

Sans II is a superb example of Hesse's craft—or, better put, it is an imposing fragment of what the complete *Sans II* was when it was displayed at the Whitney in 1968. The Refco piece is one of five now separated units that ran like a frieze across nearly twenty-two feet of wall, repeating the same arrangement of paired traylike shapes thirty times. (The other fragments are dispersed among the Whitney, a private collection, and the Saatchi Collection in London.) Cast from five gum-rubber molds, *Sans II* was Hesse's largest work. It demonstrates her interest in finding variety in repetition, in devising subtle and meditative surfaces that play with light, in creating texture and substance and form that has an organic presence. Each component seems at first slavishly to echo its predecessor, yet each finally begins to exult in the many differences that assert individuality amongst the throng. Nothing is truly repeated, and the mold is ultimately unable to constrain varied states of uniqueness.

The sculpture is indeed both delicate and fragile. Its fiberglass surface has the stiffening and brittle quality of drying skin, and in a very real sense *Sans II* is biodegrading, beginning to decompose, responding to its environment through chemical changes that have already slightly altered its color. Hesse was aware of the long-term impermanence of her objects. Her desire to move sculpture beyond traditional materials toward new and untested substances with differing properties made this quality of transience, of an object-life, something Hesse would accept and begin to incorporate into her works. JY

26
Sans II, 1968
Polyester resin
38 x 86 x 6

Eva Hesse, born Hamburg, Germany, 1936; died in New York City, 1970

GROUP SOLIDARITY
Cybernetic
Data Products

Jenny **Holzer**

Modern urban life is characterized by a kaleidoscopic consciousness. Bombarded on all sides by disconnected sights, sounds, and snippets of information, city dwellers learn to absorb, select, or often disregard the components of the sensory influx that forms the background of daily experience. Jenny Holzer takes advantage of our ability to live with such confusion, and skillfully exploits the language and techniques of advertising to question the underlying assumptions of mass communication. In her *Truisms* series, she presents a sequence of statements she described to the *New York Times Magazine* in 1989 as her version of "everything that could be right or wrong with the world expressed in the forms of people's pronouncements." The simple-sounding sentences of the *Truisms* seem to issue from some disembodied authoritarian voice. In reality, they belong to the genre of half-truths or clichés that, when unquestioned, govern private and social behavior. By assembling a collection of such thoughts, Holzer reveals the extent to which "common sense" is self-contradictory. Focusing on the clash of irreconcilable maxims, she hopes to break through the lull of background voices and inspire viewers to re-examine their own beliefs.

The *Truisms* originally were printed on sheets of colored paper which Holzer anonymously plastered all over Manhattan. Here, running continuously across an electronic signboard, they mimic the artificially generated hype of high-tech advertising. More recently, Holzer has begun to experiment with the placement of her increasingly unsettling messages on granite and marble benches and slabs where they are carved into the stone like funerary inscriptions. Holzer's work has evolved, on one hand, out of a fascination with the modes of communication pioneered by the mass media, and on the other, out of a sense of moral outrage over the passive complacency engendered by these modes.

To administer a therapeutic jolt to her viewers, Holzer has installed her work in such unexpected places as the Times Square Spectacolor board or the baggage claim area of the Las Vegas airport. In such locations, her electronic messages might, but for their problematic content, be mistaken for real advertising. She has also played with a variety of voices and tones in her signs, ranging from the hypnotic authority of Big Brother to the fearful whispers of the oppressed, the impassioned anger of the dissident, and the frustrated impotence of the powerless. Thus contradiction, displacement, and anomaly all become weapons in Holzer's attack on conventional thinking. Through them she hopes to remind her viewers of their responsibility to think for themselves. EH

27
Untitled (From *Truisms* series), 1985
Electric sign with yellow diode, ed. 2/5
5 1/2 x 30 1/2 x 4

Jenny Holzer, born Gallipolis, Ohio, 1950; lives in New York City and Hoosick, New York

Rebecca **Horn**

Machine fantasies loom large in the modern imagination. From Jules Verne and H. G. Wells to contemporary purveyors of cinema futurism and cyber-punk sci-fi, the advances of technology have been presented in terms both fearful and seductive. The kinetic sculptures of German artist Rebecca Horn embody this mixed message. A performance artist turned filmmaker and sculptor, she has long been fascinated by the notion of the body as a kind of machine. In her early work, she went so far as to turn herself into a hybrid human/machine with the addition of prosthesis-like arm and head extensions in the form of wings, horns, or masks. Her more recent sculptures, meanwhile, have a disturbingly animate quality. A motorized whip installed on the wall may snap at random intervals, a pair of brushes may flap periodically like agitated wings or spatter paint in abrupt motions against the wall.

Horn has also produced a number of room-size installations in which electric circuits leap suddenly across exposed wires or tiny hammers strike incessantly and uselessly away at the massive stone walls that confine them. Despite her reliance on motorized elements, however, Horn never dazzles us with complicated technology. Instead, she leaves her extremely rudimentary apparatuses visible, employing their very crudity to make a statement about the inhumanity of the machine.

Beetles in Conversation uses a metaphor Horn has employed on a number of occasions. The pair of South American rhinoceros beetles rest on motorized arms that fling them together periodically in a violent but unconsummated kiss. In this work, as in other pieces, there are unmistakable sexual overtones. The pent-up explosions and near misses suggest the pathos of frustrated desire and failed connection. Meanwhile, the fortuitous rhythm of the clicks that accompany the motion begins to resemble an indecipherable primitive language or code. The sense of futility invoked here recalls the work of such earlier twentieth-century artists as Jean Tinguely, who built a series of self-destructing machines, or Marcel Duchamp, whose celebrated *Large Glass* is the model for a machine fueled by the never-to-be-satisfied sexual desire of a group of bachelors for an inaccessible bride.

Thus, beneath the humorous absurdity of Horn's mechanical device, there is an undercurrent of melancholy. The machine makes a poor model for human life, the artist suggests: communication is limited and selfhood endangered by the deadened consciousness produced by the mindless repetitions and meaningless rituals of a mechanized existence. EH

28
Beetles in Conversation, 1988
Mixed media, beetles
48 x 15 x 5

Rebecca Horn, born Michelstadt, Germany, 1944; lives in Bad Konig-Zeil, West Germany

Jim **Jacobs**

Jim Jacobs' art is governed by paradox. As a young man, he was a student of John Chamberlain, who creates compelling abstract sculpture out of old crushed automobile parts. In his own work, Jacobs demonstrates that he has learned from his mentor to play on the shock of recognition we feel when the familiar is reworked in unfamiliar ways. In one body of paintings, Jacobs borrows immediately recognizable compositions from such masters of twentieth-century abstraction as Piet Mondrian, Josef Albers, and Frank Stella. However, instead of presenting them straight, Jacobs paints these icons of modern art as if he had creased and folded over their edges. With witty irreverence, he undermines the usual critical rhetoric that surrounds these works, seeing them as demonstrations of the importance of flatness and the integrity of the picture plane in modernist painting.

Kansas II comes from a subsequent series of abstract images in which Jacobs adapts the lacquer technique first developed in China many centuries ago. His compositions are based on landscape, geological formations, and aerial views of the earth inspired by vistas the artist has glimpsed while aloft in his airplane. These paintings feature gestural marks and forms whose apparent spontaneity belies the laborious nature of the lacquering process, which can involve the application of up to sixty layers of color. There is as well an odd contradiction in the application of an ancient art technique more usually associated with decorative Japanese or Chinese screens or furniture to something so obviously non-functional as modern painting.

Thus, in this work, as in his earlier folded masterworks, Jacobs encourages us to rethink rigid distinctions between tradition and innovation. Nothing is sacred, since the art forms and styles we now regard as unassailable were once themselves as daring and fresh as the playful transformations Jacobs works on them. Whether he draws his inspiration from the art of the recent or the ancient past, whether his abstractions are based on the icons of Modernism or the irregular geometry of the aerial landscape, Jacobs reminds us that art must grow and change if it is to remain a vital cultural force. EH

29
Kansas II, 1983
Lacquer on board
60 x 48 1/2

Jim Jacobs, born New York City, 1945; lives in Great Barrington, Massachusetts

ATMOSPHERE

Neil **Jenney**

How can we meaningfully characterize our complex and multi-leveled relationship to nature? In a computerized, urbanized, and socialized world, confusion and ambivalence over this issue have begun to reign, and nature, which for at least six hundred years has been a staple of artistic inquiry, has lost much of its hold on modern art. Beyond the earthwork artists of the 1960s and 1970s, some environmental activists, and curious and bracing voices like Neil Jenney's, nature is a subject contemporary art has largely abjured. But in Jenney's paintings, a threatened environment has found a sobering advocate, a seductive and wise appeal to conscience and—pun intended—to our better nature.

Atmosphere trumpets its title in bold gray letters emblazoned across a board attached to the painting's carefully handcrafted frame. The alliance of title and painted image is deeply signified; Jenney sets word and picture in a direct relation which suggests they will define and illustrate one another. Beyond that device, painting and frame interact at another, perhaps more subtle level. Jenney's painted panel, a lovely and sensuously textured field of chalk yellow that slowly and gradually evolves toward a rich violet, is rendered as if it is actually radiating light. The frame of *Atmosphere* is physically illumined by this aura, its ebony black darkness recedes a bit under this "light." The surface of Jenney's painting takes on the properties of a window, or a sort of oblong display case which we examine from our side. We regard the atmosphere as if it were enshrined in some museum, an artifact or souvenir of something remote or lost.

And that is Jenney's warning. It sounds like the most common cliché, but it is no less true: the atmosphere that surrounds us is at risk, and the results of our activities in the future will control its—and indeed, our own—survival. We live in this stuff, we breathe this ether, without it we will die. Its substance is the causal link in earthly life; its resources are our trust and its maintenance our legacy. Jenney's art, especially paintings such as this one from the *Biosphere* series, has long been a poetic but pointed rumination on our responsibilities to our planet, and on the dangers we have recklessly and thoughtlessly brought to its midst. Just beneath the beauty, right behind the mist, on the edge of a dream, a bit beyond where our eyes can see, the alarm sounds. JY

30
Atmosphere, 1985
Oil on panel
33 x 79 1/2

Neil Jenney, born Torrington, Connecticut, 1945; lives in New York City

Jasper **Johns**

Even at the moment of its execution, there was a sense that Jasper Johns's *Decoy* held a special place in the history of art. A television crew documented its creation, and the lithograph was the subject of an exhibition at Hofstra University in 1972. More than a manifestation of Johns's aesthetic vision, *Decoy* also marks the rehabilitation of printmaking as a major art form. Although printmaking had not fallen into disuse in the twentieth century, it had become a secondary skill, regularly practiced only by graphic-arts specialists. Painting was the chosen medium of artists such as the Abstract Expressionists, many of whom were impatient with the measured pace required in creating prints; they saw the repetitive and reproductive character of printmaking as distanced from the immediacy of more direct media. The opening of progressive print workshops, such as U.L.A.E. (Universal Limited Art Editions) on Long Island, where *Decoy* was made, helped change this bias. By the 1960s, artists such as Helen Frankenthaler, Roy Lichtenstein, Claes Oldenburg, Robert Rauschenberg, and Frank Stella regularly tested their skills in printmaking.

Johns's *Decoy* is an autobiographical print, a mini-retrospective of his career. Across the bottom of the sheet, Johns has placed faded echoes of his earlier etchings: a flag, flashlight, Savarin coffee can, numbers, and Ballantine ale cans line up in a sequence that starts to repeat itself. (The X through each indicates that these images are derived from their original etching plates, cancelled by the artist after their printing run.) Above this, across a washy black sea of printer's ink, stenciled names of colors revolve around another enshrined ale can. The print is topped with a pale aqua area, out of which emerges a rendering of a plaster cast of human legs. These images come together to form an elusive and mysterious melange; naming and numbering Johns's components brings no conclusions, offering only specificity in the midst of pools of ambiguity. *Decoy* is a personal album, a cachepot of memories, and functions as its title suggests if analyzed too restrictively.

As a lithograph, *Decoy* broke one more tradition in art. Artists like Johns usually made prints to document and disseminate ideas they had already explored in painting. *Decoy* has the opposite history: *after* its execution, Johns made two paintings that replicate this print, and serve as its variations. The tables indicating a hierarchy of artistic media, with printmaking playing a subservient role, were now decidedly and emphatically turned. JY

31
Decoy, 1971
Lithograph, ed. 49/55
41 x 29

Jasper Johns, born
Augusta, Georgia, 1930;
lives in New York City

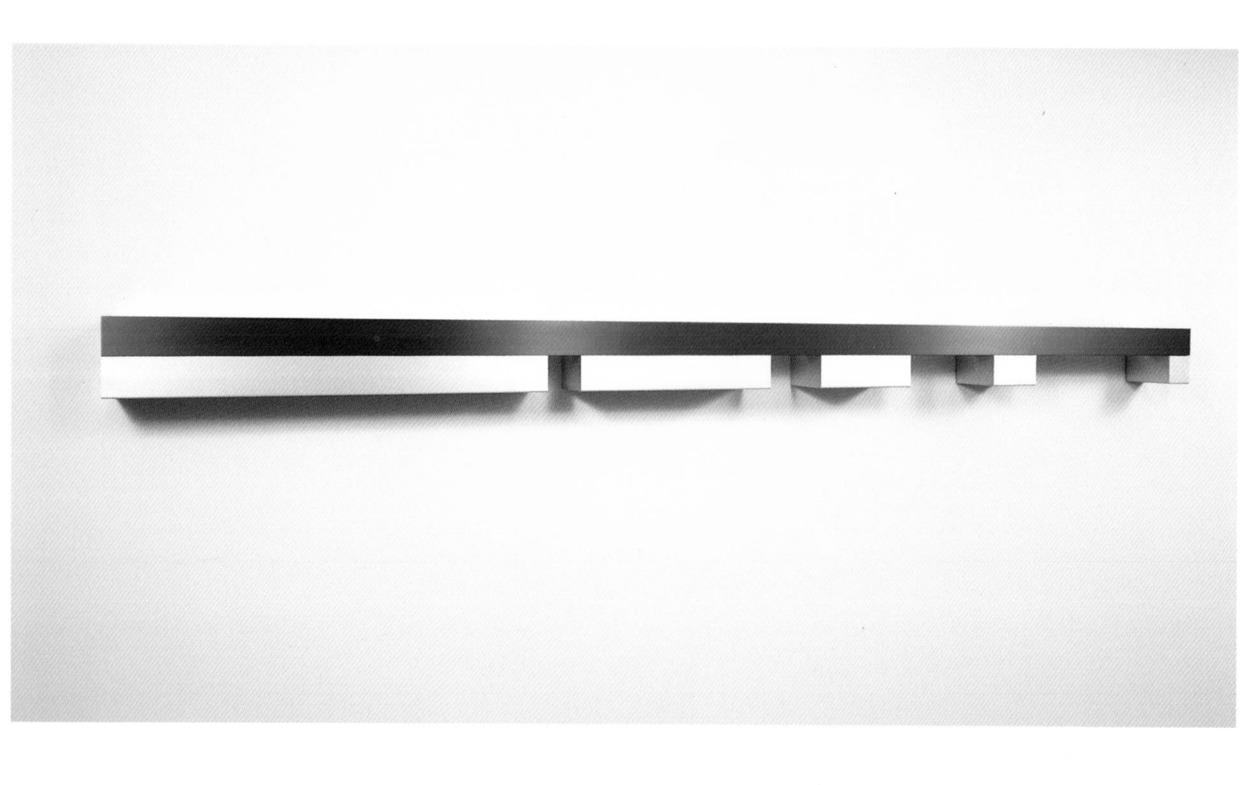

Donald **Judd**

Donald Judd is in many ways the quintessential Minimalist. His austerely elegant aesthetic has its origins in the early 1960s, a moment in contemporary art when an almost puritanical fervor for clarity and fact swept the art world. Judd was no small part of that revolution, both in his sculpture and in his writings which made the case for an art purged of metaphor and illusion. Although he began as a painter, Judd quickly abandoned that medium for sculpture, which, he believed, was less susceptible to the temptation to fool the eye or create an illusion of space.
His sculptures are models of lucidity—simple cubes and boxes, often arranged in modular series, and created out of such clean, finished, industrial materials as plywood boards, sheets of Plexiglas, iron, steel, or brass. They challenge the traditional focus of sculpture on craftsmanship, hand finish, and uniqueness. Judd believed that art had left these ideals behind as it entered a new era of standardization and scientific objectivity.

Despite the somewhat forbidding nature of his rhetoric, the work Judd has produced throughout his long career has an appealing simplicity. Following a principle he labeled "polarization," each of his sculptures exhibits a tension between two disparate aspects—a juxtaposition of dissimilar materials, for instance, or a play between open and closed volumes, or a contrast between vivid colors and spare forms. In this untitled work, one can see such polarization both in the alternating rhythm of the closed boxes and the open gaps that separate them and in the contrast between the dull metallic upper strip and the brilliant blue of the aluminum boxes below. As a result of this interplay between form and materials, Judd's sculptures may be extremely simple, but they are never boring.

Despite the messianic zeal with which Judd and his colleagues promoted Minimalism as the culmination of modern art history, subsequent developments in contemporary art have demonstrated that the urge for metaphor and illusion have never been entirely quashed. Nevertheless, the art and philosophy Judd and others advanced more than two decades ago continue to exert a tremendous influence over younger artists. Many of the works in this collection would be unimaginable without Minimalism. To inhabitants of the confusing world of the 1990s, moreover, it seems that the sense of conviction and certitude embodied in works like this can be oddly comforting. EH

32
Untitled (Progression),
1979
Aluminum
6 x 6 x 110 1/2

Donald Judd, born
Excelsior, Missouri, 1928;
lives in New York City
and Marfa, Texas

Anselm **Kiefer**

Among the European artists causing a reconsideration of the possibilities of art in our day, few present as bracing and wide-ranging a vision as Anselm Kiefer. When his art began to be shown in the United States in the early 1980s, it spoke of concerns not approached here for a long time. Kiefer, it was clear, believed in the ability of art not only to carry narrative and symbolic meaning but also to comment on issues of the most complex moral import. His roughly scumbled, tortuous, and aggressive images dealt with matters as serious and profound as his determination to confront and, in a sense, expiate his own German heritage by pictorially analyzing the legacy of Nazism. With the sobering belief that an experience of art can act as a form of emotional purgative, Kiefer's immersion into the seas of history was a gesture of boldness that caught and transfixed the attention of the art world.

Kiefer senses the potential for drama in the world around him, and *Mast* had its origins in a black-and-white photograph of an embankment at the side of a road. The artist must have been struck by the bold diagonal that crosses the image from lower left to upper right, by the forceful way that diagonal is echoed by the electrical power lines hanging above, and further, how all this is bisected by the powerful vertical element of the telephone pole. Kiefer looked at this photograph, and recognized how it could be altered to take on a completely different profile and meaning. By blowing up the photo, and by covering parts of its surface with an emulsion of paint and other materials, Kiefer restructures the image, seeing in it now the silhouette of a massive and gloomy sailing ship. The embankment becomes a prow, the telephone pole a mast, the power lines its rigging, and the road the sea through which the ship sails.

This metamorphosis from roadway into something that suggests the brooding vessel of Richard Wagner's Flying Dutchman intensifies visual experience, and expands its possibilities. The transubstantiation is hard won; the molten lead and battered areas looking stained and rusted on *Mast's* surface remind us that, as in alchemy, this change from one state to another is not easy. Kiefer's intense mediation transforms one way of passage into another; something is recovered and revealed in his sensitivity to the realms of meaning that exist just beyond the world of sight, in those places that beg for a closer look. JY

33
Mast, 1984-85
Lead, acrylic, lacquer, emulsion over photograph on board
41 1/4 x 27 1/2

Anselm Kiefer, born Donaueschingen, Germany, 1945; lives in Hornbach, West Germany

Komar and Melamid

34
Thirty Years Ago 1953, 1982-83
Oil on canvas
72 x 47

Vitali Komar, born Moscow, 1943; lives in New York City
Aleksandr Melamid, born Moscow, 1945; lives in Jersey City, New Jersey

In *Thirty Years Ago*, two teenage students merge in a riotous embrace at what appears to be a landing in a school stairwell. Beneath the stern and watchful gaze of a portrait of Joseph Stalin, the exuberance of youth is served; something has caused these youngsters to ignore decorum in a demonstration of their insuppressible excitement and joy. Painted in 1983, what we witness may be an event that occurred around 5 March 1953, the day that Joseph Vissarionovich Dzhugashvil, who named himself Stalin (made of steel), died. Although official Soviet propaganda of the time portrayed a nation consumed in grief, there may well have been the sort of displays of nascent hope and liberation we see illustrated here.

Two small boys who lived in Moscow at the time might have remembered that moment. Vitali Komar and Aleksandr Melamid would later meet in the early 1960s in an anatomy class at Moscow's Strogonov Institute for Art and Design, and would team up for good in 1965. Their training was in the blandest form of Soviet realist art, tried and true illustrators' techniques that served the decorative and didactic needs of the state. But a Soviet system unaware of the perestroika to come was unprepared for the infectious energy of these two artists. Their subsequent send-ups of Soviet—and Western—political mythologies led them to be seen as crazy "refuseniks," and facilitated their emigration to the West in 1977.

Komar and Melamid's collaboration is a complete one. Both are involved in the design and execution of each picture, and it is impossible to separate their individual hands. Their predilection for clear narrative and a painstakingly realist style seems at first a throwback to an earlier time in art. But their use of realism in images like *Thirty Years Ago* is not without its subversive quality. Komar and Melamid sense the power of narrative directness, and are well trained in the ways realism can be subtly channeled toward rhetorical and propagandistic ends. Here, however, in their charged and sometimes whimsical world, they, and not the state, will write the revisionist histories and give voice to those whom it is often denied. Did what we see in *Thirty Years Ago* actually happen? Perhaps not, but the art of Komar and Melamid convinces us that if it had, it would have looked very much like this. JY

JEFF KOONS
EXPLOIT THE MASSES
BANALITY
MUST

JEFF KOONS

J E F F K O O N S
SONNABEND • NEW YORK • MAX HETZLER • KOLN DONALD YOUNG • CHICAGO
PHOTO GREG GORMAN

J E F F K O O N S
SONNABEND • NEW YORK MAX HETZLER • KÖLN DONALD YOUNG • CHICAGO

Jeff **Koons**

35
Jeff Koons Art Magazine Ads, 1989
Four lithographs, ed. 1/50
each 36 x 28

Jeff Koons, born York, Pennsylvania, 1955; lives in New York City

Jeff Koons was planning his next exhibition, which would occur in November 1988. As befitting the art world's hottest and most hotly debated young celebrity, whose work was fetching astronomical prices, the exhibition would open at three major galleries simultaneously—Donald Young in Chicago, Sonnabend in New York, and Galerie Max Hetzler in Cologne. At each site, Koons would show examples of his most recent limited-edition sculptures, including life-size plaster and ceramic gilt statues of Michael Jackson and Buster Keaton, corny cherubic angels, bubble-gum nudes, London bobbies, and teddy bears. Nothing could be too trite, too devalued or kitsch to escape this unapologetic enshrinement of irony. Like a Disney-esque Midas, Koons would touch the emptiest clichés of popular culture and bring them into the hallowed halls of art, where intelligent people would expend huge sums for them. And they did.

But how to advertise this event, how to whet the market's appetite for the forthcoming spectacle? It is customary for galleries representing artists of Koons's stature to run a spate of ads in major art magazines. The approach in these ads is usually a restrained one—the artist's name is set in simple block letters above the gallery logo, or a reproduction of an artwork to be exhibited is included as a kind of appetizer. But this wouldn't do for the crown prince of controversy; it would not be sufficiently august and complex to herald his 1988 arrival.

Koons's recent art is a descent into bitter wisdoms. It mockingly exposes the tenuous balance between low culture and high art, it genially embraces the complete ascendancy of big money in contemporary art, it grins gleefully as it seeks altars to befoul. It is a cunning whisper of corruption resting just beneath an imperviously gilded veneer. And the artist's role in all of this? In the four rather expensive ads Koons created for *Artforum, Art in America, Arts,* and *Flash Art,* he dutifully fulfills whatever fantasies of an artist we might possess. Koons is happy to role-play, to present himself as avatar and sex machine, culture god and loving mentor, child of nature and possessor of mystic truths. He posits himself as product, a medium of transcendence with value independent of his artwork. And, like any other Hollywood hero, Koons tugs our sleeve shamelessly to expose himself, while truly revealing nothing. JY

Willi **Kopf**

36
Untitled, 1987
Pasteboard; five units
each 6 1/4 x 12 1/2 x 9 1/2

Willi Kopf, born
Rothis-Vorarlberg, Austria,
1949; lives in Vienna

Europe has always had a rather ambivalent attitude toward Minimalism. On one hand, museums and galleries there have, since the 1960s, been indefatigable in their interest; artists such as Sol LeWitt, Carl Andre, Dan Flavin, and Richard Serra have found some of their most significant successes and acclaim on European soil. But, while Minimalism has been held in very high regard by curators, dealers, and collectors, it has not been widely practiced by European artists. There may have been something in the aesthetic rigors of Minimalism, in aspects of its purist doctrine and emphasis on abstraction that was congenial to Americans while uninteresting to European artists. Viewed from a several-thousand-year tradition of figural art, some of the ascetic qualities of modern American art turned out to be alien to a European sensibility.

But by the late 1980s, the situation changed. Willi Kopf is part of a new generation of European artists, and this untitled work fulfills all the litmus tests we might apply to it as a minimalist monument. It is sculpture. It is abstract, unemotional, made of a modern, postindustrial material in which color is of secondary significance. It is about measure, perception, formal and sequential arrangements, and is the result of a predetermined system. Attached to the wall in a reserved manner, it reflects architectural qualities. Its silhouette is dependent on our position in space. And it is severe, rigorous, unbending, and hermetic, extremely impassive and secretive, an intellectual statement demanding a sober analysis.

Each of the units comprising *Untitled* is identical in size and shape. It is within their respective contours that difference is introduced: a seemingly arbitrary patterning is created by the incorporation of slightly darker pieces of pasteboard. But does what occurs on a unit's surface have any effect inside? Are the units hollow? Why this sequence? Why pasteboard? Should this piece be read left to right? Is anything being developed here? Could it be continued in infinite variation? Answers to questions like these are elusive, but what is not is the quality of visual intrigue Kopf's work can excite. In a very surprising way, the longer one examines *Untitled's* components, the more they begin to evoke thoughts of Henri Matisse's relief sculpture series known as *The Back*. Sweet are the uses of permutation. JY

Jannis **Kounellis**

37
Untitled, 1987
Steel, wood, wax, nails
70 x 71

Jannis Kounellis, born
Piraeus, Greece, 1936;
lives in Rome

Born in Greece and now living in Italy, Jannis Kounellis is linked by his ethnic background to the long history of Mediterranean culture. He also belongs, however, to the postwar generation for whom the comforts of tradition and cultural unity were forever shattered by the ravages of the Second World War. His art reflects this sense of loss and fragmentation, evoking a world that can never again be made whole.

To this end, he works with a variety of "non-art" materials, employing natural substances such as burnished gold, coal, wax, and lead and such common weathered objects as scraps of ragged wood and broken table legs. He arranges these elements in assemblage sculptures and room-sized installations which evoke the passage of time and the ephemeral nature of human existence. At times, he has incorporated fragments of plaster casts, suggesting the fracturing of the classical past. In other works, he incorporates fire as a metaphor for death and rebirth by rigging up gas jets that shoot flames across space and leave soft shadows of sooty residue on the wall.

In this untitled work, Kounellis makes one of his frequent uses of the shelf. Massive and discolored, lined with an assortment of fragmentary objects and scraps of building material, the shelf becomes a kind of repository of memory. The items arranged along its length bear marks of some previous existence and make metaphoric reference to ancient relics or shards of the sort uncovered in an archaeological dig. In many of his shelf works, Kounellis plays the physical properties of his elements against each other. Here, the lumps of yellow wax seem soft and pliable, bringing to mind the properties of fat or flesh, while the steel beams are cold and unyielding. Scraps of weathered wood piled atop each other recall a pre-industrial past, as if salvaged from a world that had not yet become rigidly standardized. Using ordinary materials which have been touched by time, Kounellis reminds us that loss, alteration, and imperfection are inescapable facts of human life. His work forms a melancholy elegy to Western civilization's vain dreams of control. EH

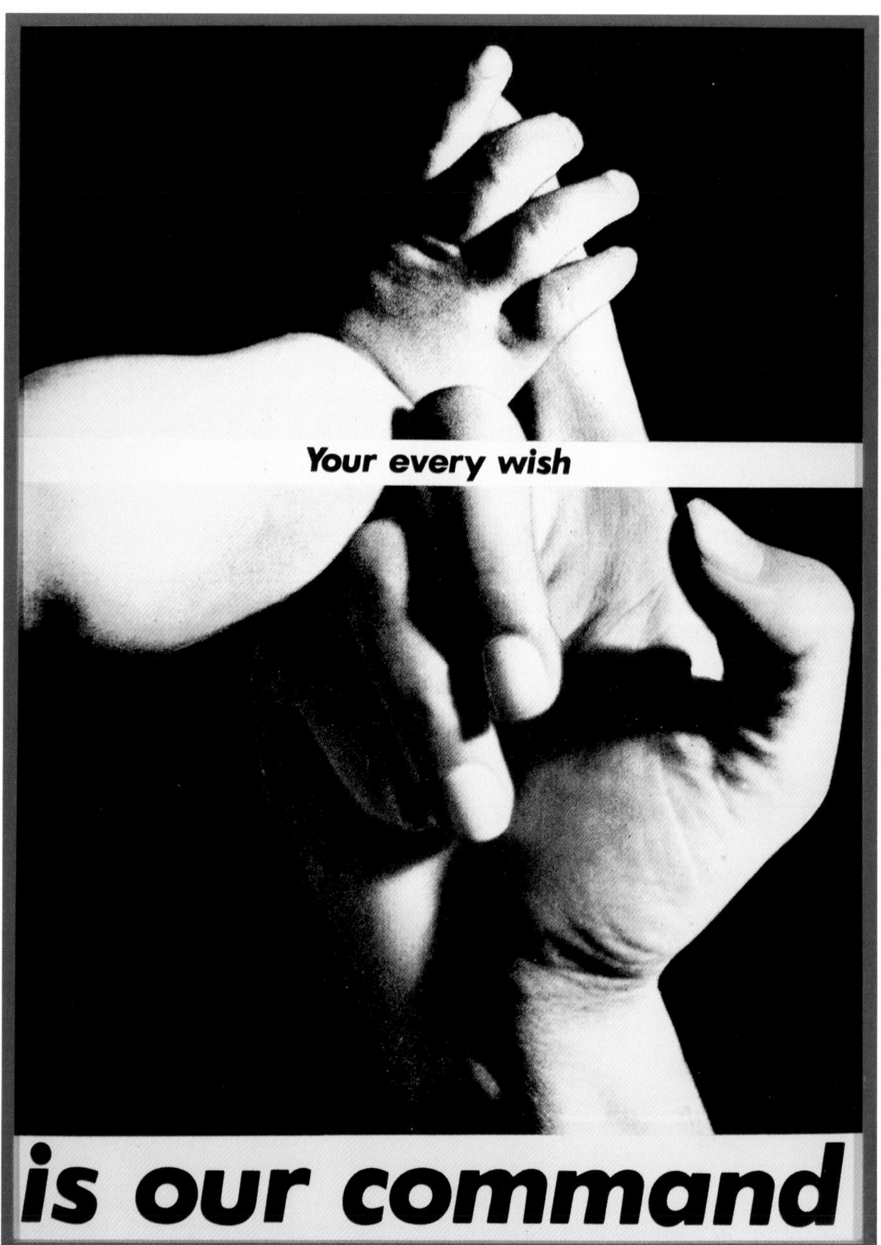
Your every wish
is our command

Barbara **Kruger**

38
Untitled (Your Every Wish Is Our Command), 1982
Unique photo montage
56 x 40 1/2

Barbara Kruger, born Newark, New Jersey, 1945; lives in New York City

Public service announcements, television commercials, and magazine ads tend to share a common persuasive tone. Subliminally, we understand that the voice of authority behind them is male, and that the audience of consumers he addresses is, more often than not, female. Barbara Kruger, who worked for eleven years as photo editor and designer for Condé Nast, knows better than most how the mass media convey their messages. In her photo collages, she attempts to short-circuit that process. Her works have a deliberately posterlike quality and combine black-and-white photographic reproductions culled from archives, old magazines, and how-to handbooks with striking graphic mottoes. The relationship between image and text is always more suggestive than explanatory, and the printed declarations themselves have a vaguely propagandistic tone.

One of the important twists Kruger works on the standard advertising format is the reversal of genders associated with speaker and audience. In texts like "We won't play nature to your culture," "We are your elaborate holes," or, as here, "Your every wish is our command," the speaker is female, the viewer presumably male. Thus, one point of her work is to challenge, by making them explicit, the ubiquitous and covert messages in our culture that reinforce female passivity. Kruger's choice of images contributes to this challenge. Enigmatic and removed from their original contexts, they present puzzles that cannot be fully decoded. Here, a child's tiny hand grasps a woman's finger. Combined with the text, it suggests the woman's conventional role as a caretaker who puts the needs and desires of others before her own. Is the child her charge or her master? Is this relationship healthy or destructive? With this work, Kruger brings into public view and opens for public debate the social contract that assigns roles of authority to some, of dependence and service to others.

Kruger's work tends to revolve around three themes—the power relationships between men and women, the subtle persuasions of consumerism, and the social and economic role of art in our culture. In each case, her focus is on breaking through rigid role definitions which keep the status quo in place. Borrowing the language of advertising, she uses the tools of our culture's authoritarian voices to liberate us from their grip. EH

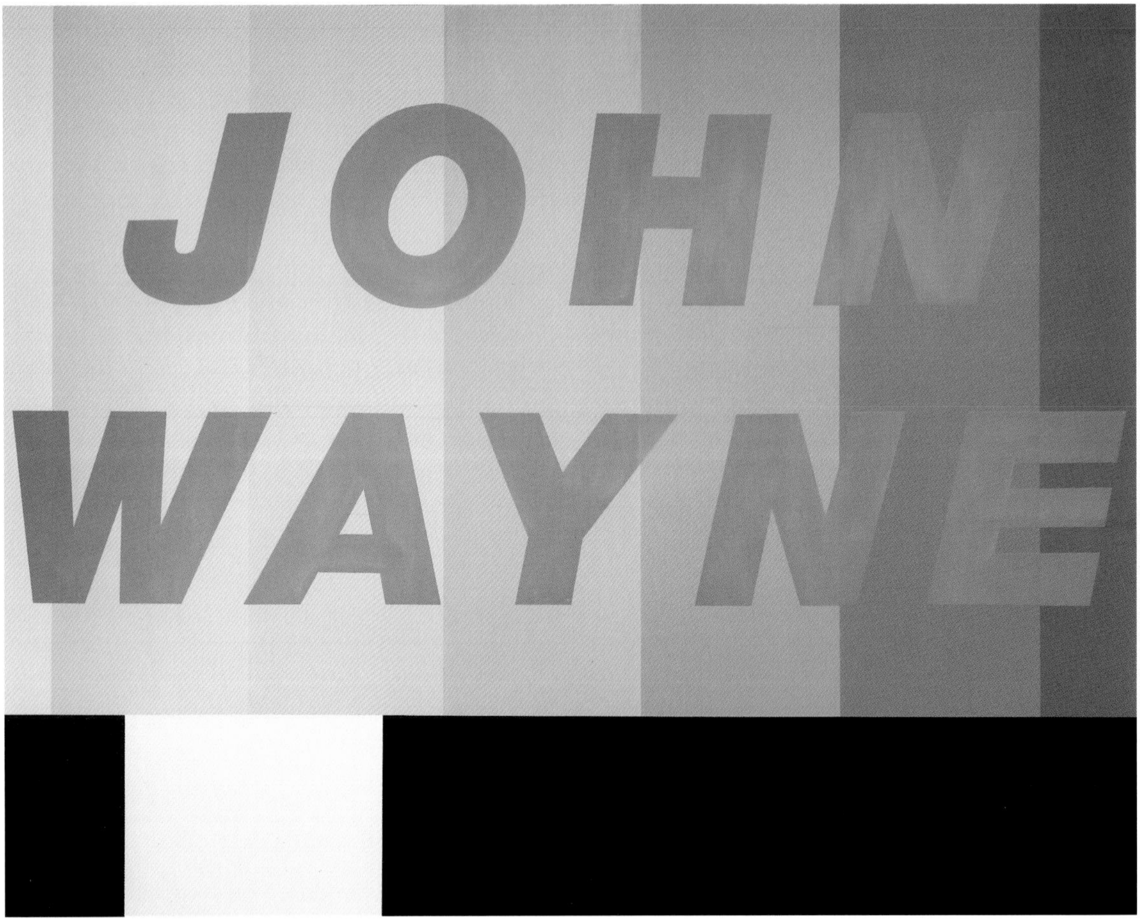

JOHN
WAYNE

Annette **Lemieux**

Since the 1960s, many artists have been intrigued by the tactics of commercial art, particularly as spectacularly manifested in the promotion of products through advertising. Artists saw in the methods of Madison Avenue the skilled employment of an economy of means, and how subtle but manipulative assaults on consumers were achieved by straightforward and direct pictorial clarity. Today, Annette Lemieux's cool and reserved evocation of John Wayne banks on our instant recognition of its subject matter, our immediate—if arguably superficial—sense of its meaning. We feel we know the many things John Wayne has come to mean: bedrock American virtues, man conquering the savage West, honor, machismo, duty, grit-your-teeth-and-pass-the-ammo. John Wayne represents a modern archetypal myth, one of the core fables of the American male.

And he means fantasy. There was of course no such man as John Wayne, just an actor named Marion Michael Morrison from Winterset, Iowa. He drifted to California, went to college, worked as a stuntman and bit actor, and eventually came to embody one of our culture's deepest dreams about itself. It is that dream and its aura of male posturing that Lemieux subtly undercuts. She presents John Wayne like some blaring banner headline, in gold brown capitals spanning her canvas from edge to edge, popping forth from an anonymous abstract gray background which is reminiscent of a TV test pattern. The powerful graphic arrangement of the letters of his name is as effective here as it would be in any ad, or on any movie marquee. Lemieux, in an almost prescient manner, knows that we will do the rest, that this spare image will mean as much and probably more than if she had shown the man in action, astride a horse, or leading his troops into battle. John Wayne becomes not a person but a logo, a product for our cinematic and mythic consumption, with dependable and constant meaning.

This condition is precisely what Lemieux's painting seeks to analyze and deflect. Her work asks us to think about our beliefs and to question whether they are based on anything deeper than media manipulation. In her choice of John Wayne, Lemieux especially calls to account our culture's obsession with concepts of fame and our willingness to sacrifice difficult realities for the ease of fantasy at any juncture. Lemieux senses that we are interested in the dream of quick and one-dimensional solutions to complex problems, a tendency full of its own special dangers. JY

39
John Wayne, 1986
Oil on canvas
72 x 92

Annette Lemieux, born Norfolk, Virginia, 1957; lives in Boston

Sherrie **Levine**

This is only a test. But among the things placed at risk in Sherrie Levine's work are some of the very values and precepts that can define the essence of art. That's the way it has been with this artist since she first attracted notice in the early 1980s. Levine was then exhibiting her photographs and small painted copies after pre-existing works by masters of modern art history such as Walker Evans, Fernand Léger, Franz Marc, and Piet Mondrian. Levine defused her sources with bold mimicry, presenting her appropriations with a deadpan straightforwardness and challenging the hierarchical structures that enshrine the authentic, one-of-a-kind "masterpiece" above all else. Her reproductions of reproductions used for their source not the original artworks, but illustrations of them taken from textbooks and magazines. This created images of irony that seemed to hover between homage and coy parody. Through the mid 1980s, Levine continued this persistent and multi-leveled inquiry into academic concepts of value and artistic greatness, and the patriarchal power structures played out in their name.

More recently, Levine has turned her attention to other artistic traditions, and in several series she has probed the methods and aspirations of modern "hard-edged" abstraction. *Untitled (Lead Checks/Lead Chevrons: 11)* appears to be a checker- or chessboard placed above a backgammon board. Levine's title for the work, however, emphasizes its geometrical design and articulation, rather than its potential for use. Despite our recognition of their source, we seem to be asked to scan these boards as pure and pristine pattern. A different game is being essayed here; in their present vertical state the gameboards are nonfunctional, divorced from their original purpose. These are no longer games awaiting players, but imponderable designs awaiting viewers. The object now stands like a wall sculpture, a trophy or shield of aesthetic endgame, and Levine's application of the dry, dusty casein over a somewhat battered lead surface reinforces the imposing sense of this being a rendered thing. Abstract art and an item of vernacular use just elude coming together in uneasy union, and we vacillate in the interval.

In that interval is the test that interests Levine. We begin to analyze and question our own expectations of what art should be, and how we should respond to finding those expectations challenged and exposed. Our traditional hopes for discourse and/or revelation in art are undercut, or at the very least are cunningly redirected, and replaced by a wariness that opens up new and possibly vexing potentials for art. JY

40
Untitled (Lead Checks/ Lead Chevron: 11), 1988
Casein on lead
40 x 20

Sherrie Levine, born Hazleton, Pennsylvania, 1947; lives in New York City

Sol **LeWitt**

Although he is associated with the rational aesthetic of Minimalism by viewers familiar with his stark white cube sculptures, serial grids, and rigorously plotted wall drawings, Sol LeWitt is also fascinated with the mystical side of geometry. Nowhere is this clearer than in the richly tactile wall paintings that have formed an important part of his output since 1980. These paintings are connected to his earlier work in a variety of ways. Their focus on pure geometric shapes—cubes, pyramids, and rectangles—is consistent with LeWitt's long-term interest in the mathematical analysis of form. The format of the wall drawing itself goes back to the artist's early manifestoes in the 1960s, promoting a conceptual art in which, as he put it, "The idea becomes a machine that makes the art."

In conformity with that notion, LeWitt conceived of "drawings" that were merely sets of detailed instructions about the length, width, and disposition of a set of lines which could then be transferred to a wall surface by any competent assistant. In these works, LeWitt employed mathematics and geometry as visual embodiments of pure mind. He described his intentions in his "Paragraphs on Conceptual Art," published in *Artforum* in 1967: "This kind of art is not theoretical or illustrative of theories; it is intuitive, it is involved with all types of mental processes and it is purposeless. It is usually free from the dependence on the skill of the artist as a craftsman."

While he continues to work in these rather ascetic modes, a wall painting like *Multiple Asymmetrical Pyramids* reintroduces the sensuous, allowing the artist to indulge in an almost voluptuous feeling for color and material. Eschewing the strict black, white, and unmodulated primary colors that characterize his earlier work, LeWitt here uses rich earthy tones which reach outside the world of abstract geometry and into a sensory experience of nature. He also imbues the forms with a physical presence, basing them on isometric projections which provide a three-dimensional appearance. Enlarged to a grand scale, these pyramids assume an iconic presence and bring to mind cabalistic symbols and ritualistic monuments. Thus, geometry is no longer merely an analytic tool or a mental symbol. Instead, it assumes connections with human history and physical experience. Mysterious yet rational, sensuous yet cerebral, this seductive composition reminds us that mind and body are linked in ways we cannot always fathom. EH

41
Multiple Asymmetrical Pyramids, 1987
Ink, pencil wall drawing
110 x 341 overall

Sol LeWitt, born Hartford, Connecticut, 1928; lives in Chester, Connecticut and Spoleto, Italy

Donald **Lipski**

42
Xalupax, 1985
Mixed-media installation
variable dimensions

Donald Lipski, born
Chicago, 1947; lives in
New York City

An ongoing theme in modern art is the flirtation between art and life. Of the many forms it has taken, one of the most enduring is the transformation of ordinary objects into works of art. There are, for example, Marcel Duchamp's "ready-mades"—those snow shovels, bicycle wheels, and urinals magically transmuted into art by the artist's word; Pablo Picasso's famous bull's head, created from a bicycle seat and upturned handlebars; and Joseph Cornell's magical boxes, crammed with bits of poetic rubbish. These precursors lie behind Donald Lipski's curious assemblage sculptures. His raw materials are the most unremarkable sort of everyday items—nail scissors, wrenches, toothbrushes, eyeglasses, nails, soup spoons, test tubes—but when he is finished with them they have become mysteriously animate paradoxes.

Generally Lipski's alterations are extremely modest. He may do nothing more than arrange three pairs of eyeglasses to form a triangle, for instance, or wrap the tines of a fork in wire. At times he is apparently inspired by a similarity in form, as when a coiled bottle brush becomes a kind of primitive crustacean. In other works, the impulse seems to be a negation of the object's ordinary function, as when he encases a cigar in plastic or dips a fork in plaster.

In Lipski's world, objects lose their normal meanings and are haunted by only the barest memory of their previous lives. Scattered as they are here across a wide wall, they begin to resemble a catalogue of archaeological finds whose specific purposes and cultural meanings have been long forgotten. As a result, they inspire us to regard our culture anew, from the viewpoint of an outsider. We wonder, is this all that would remain of us in some unimaginable future?

In a discussion of his work with Wade Saunders for *Art in America* in 1985, Lipski suggested another interpretation. He referred to his whimsical assemblages as "art charms," noting that the word "charm" suggests "something that has actual magic in it." This magic, one guesses, is the magic of the imagination, which can coax poetry out of the simplest arrangement of glass tubes or pencils, and remind us that reality is only boring if we allow it to be. EH

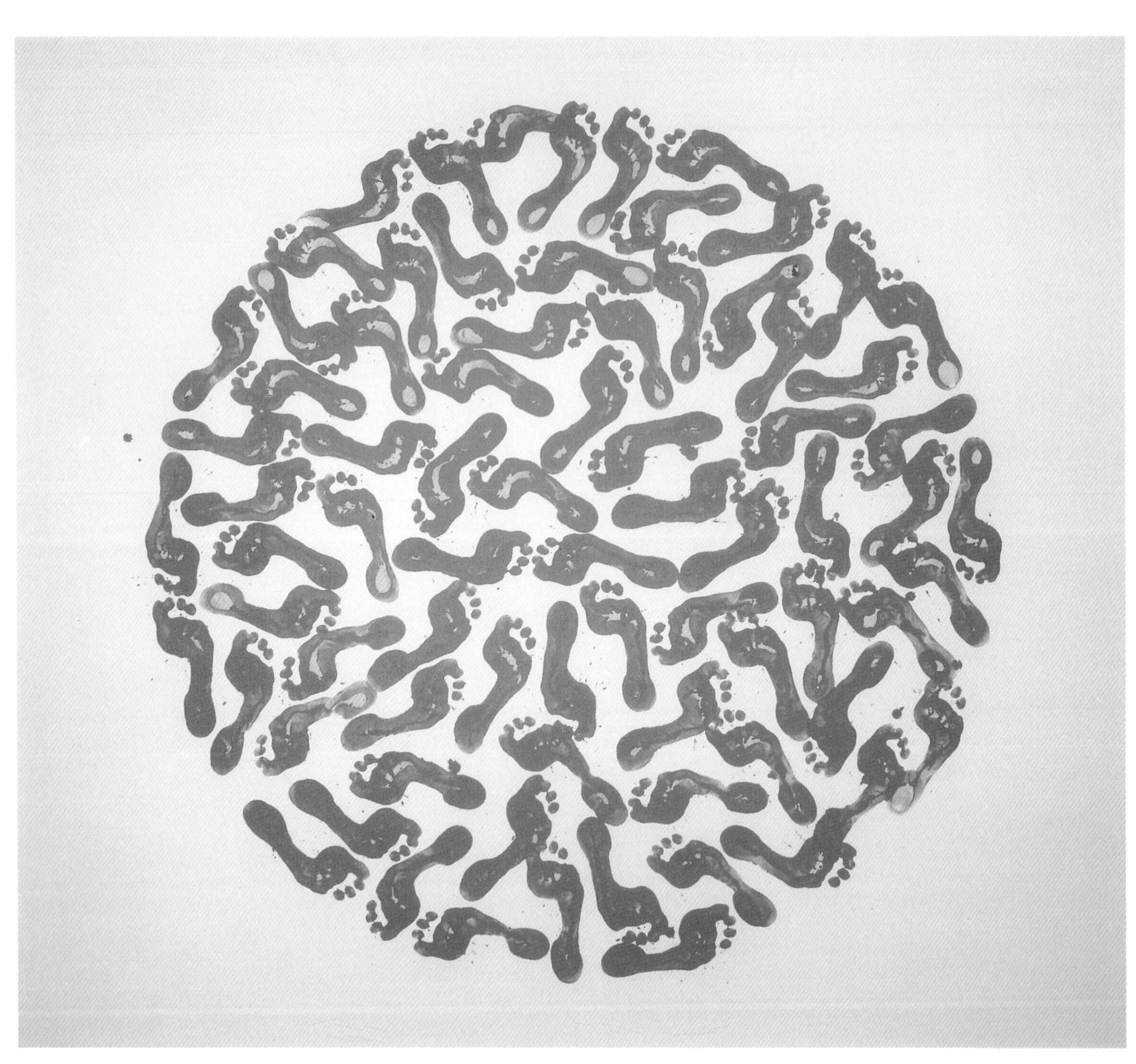

Richard **Long**

43
Mud Foot Circle, 1985
River Avon mud on paper laid on board
88 x 79

Richard Long, born Bristol, England, 1945; lives in Bristol

For most inhabitants of the industrialized world of the late twentieth century, undefiled nature is more often a cultural memory or nostalgic dream than a first-hand experience. Not so for British artist Richard Long. He seeks out the remote and still unpeopled corners of the world for the purpose of creating what he calls "walking sculptures." Long's art, or those objects he displays in galleries and museums, consists of souvenirs or photographic documentation of his solitary treks through remote landscapes of rural England or Ireland, the Australian outback, Peru, or Tibet. Such documents may include maps tracing his path, photographs taken en route, stone circles or piles of branches which recall the prehistoric mounds or steles he passes on his way. In a more profound way, however, Long's art is the journey itself, an experience which is his alone and can only be suggested by the artifacts he brings back.

Treading gently over the landscape, Long leaves behind only simple markers—heaps of stones, a swath cut through the grass—as traces of his passage. He has often been linked to a group of artists who, in the mid 1960s and seventies, created monumental "earthworks" in remote sites in the American landscape. Long is uncomfortable with this association, however, because he objects to the aggressively proprietorial stance toward nature these projects imply. He has remarked to critic Suzi Gablik, whose book posed the question *Has Modernism Failed?* (1984), "To walk in the Himalayas...is to touch the earth lightly...and has more personal physical commitment, than an artist who plans a large earthwork which is then made by bulldozers. I admire the spirit of the American Indian more than its contemporary land artists. I prefer to be a custodian of nature not an exploiter of it....I want to do away with nuclear weapons, not make art that can withstand them."

Mud Foot Circle is a work in keeping with this spirit. Composed of mud footprints arranged to form a perfect circle, this work exists both as an abstract pattern, lovely in its own right, and a record of the dancelike movements made by the artist as he created it. Like the modest piles of rocks Long arranges along his path as he makes his walks, this circle has the flavor of a prehistoric artifact. In simple yet unmistakable terms, it recalls humanity's essential connection to the earth and warns against the tendency to think ourselves grander than nature. EH

Mark **Luyten**

Since its break with realism and tradition in the mid nineteenth century, modern art has carried on a problematic relationship with history. Extolling the virtues of progress and the new, artists have often had difficulty admitting their own continuity with the past, preferring to deal with art history in terms of parody or rejection. The work of Belgian artist Mark Luyten takes a more generous approach, acknowledging both our distance from and our often thwarted longing for the lost worlds of previous centuries.

Luyten's paintings and drawings are composed of discrete parts—reproductions of eighteenth-century portraits or landscapes, black-and-white photographs of lonely mountaintops or architectural monuments, and dark earthy rectangles whose rough texture is built up of a mixture of acrylic and sand—arranged sparingly against a white background. Sometimes he includes phrases borrowed from poetry of the late nineteenth and early twentieth century. But instead of using these disparate elements to comment on the incoherence of contemporary experience or the breakdown of old ways of picturing reality, Luyten employs them as spurs to memory and imagination. He intends them to operate as visual poems in which images play off each other, suggesting metaphors and sparking further associations.

In the series of works to which *Intermezzo* belongs, Luyten mixes images of art, industry, and nature, suggesting their interconnections and interdependence. Here he explores the visual resemblance between the wind-filled sails of great merchant ships and the ribbed vault of a medieval of cathedral, in the process making reference to the disparate realms of matter and spirit, commerce and religion. Meanwhile, the rich gray-black expanse of the sandy rectangle conjures the spirit of nature, thereby bringing the far-flung aspirations and ambitions suggested by the other images literally back to earth. In such works, archival photographs of unspoiled nature and premodern architecture and reproductions from art history serve as traces of worlds to which we remain connected only through historical memory. Weaving together strands from multiple sources, Luyten makes us aware of the diverse pasts submerged within our present. EH

44
Intermezzo, 1987
Mixed media on paper
59 1/2 x 39

Mark Luyten, born
Antwerp, Belgium, 1955;
lives in Antwerp

Robert **Mangold**

Minimalist painters—such as Jo Baer, Brice Marden, Agnes Martin, and Robert Ryman—have each evolved personal and highly tuned responses to a particular set of problems. How, for example, after what was seen as the emotional excesses of Abstract Expressionism, could painting recapture a sense of order and structure? How, accepting the premise that for painting to be modern it had to be abstract and reduced to its basic elements, could it still carry meaning and authority? And how could sequences of squares, lines, and bands of color speak of authorship and intelligence?

Minimalism's great significance is it did all these things, and very much more. It taught a surprised art world that even severe abstract systems and predetermined pictorial strategies could be personal and idiosyncratic, that even within hard-edged abstraction an individual vision could render drama and—dare one say it?—excitement. At first glance, Robert Mangold's *A Square and a 90 Degree Arc with Three Rectangles (Red)* seems the rarely achieved perfect merging of title and image; every word finds its visual equivalent across this painted surface. But does it? The painting certainly appears much more orange than red, and just how many rectangles are there? The whole painting is a rectangle, itself composed of three rectangular masonite panels, and the superimposed drawing of the square creates at least two—arguably three—more rectangles, to total six or seven. The square looks as if it were drawn freehand, and it's curious how it and the line of the arc stop and start again as they cross each masonite edge. The arc seems squeezed at the top right, as if it had to be bent a little to fit into its shape.

Such observations are more than just aimless argumentation; they respond precisely to Mangold's aspirations. Positing one thing and then subtly undercutting it can cause a viewer to analyze more closely the relationships of parts to a whole. Mangold keeps us alert, and asks us to stay suspicious and wary of the endless variations that crop up even within what appear to be the most rigid structures. His art tests perception through permutation, enhancing and extending its possibilities. Mangold finally gives modern systems of order a decidedly human face; in this, he takes his place in a very long and rich tradition. JY

45
A Square and a 90 Degree Arc with Three Rectangles (Red), 1977
Acrylic, pencil on masonite
20 x 42

Robert Mangold, born North Tonawanda, New York, 1937; lives in Washingtonville, New York

Robert **Mapplethorpe**

Separated only by a camera and its lens, two of the most controversial artists of their time stare toward one another. One is Andy Warhol, "the Prince of Pop," trickster and superstar, the cultural investigator of the highest sort who himself became a cultural icon, the scrutinizer who here accepted being scrutinized. The photographer is Robert Mapplethorpe, around whom extraordinary and vitriolic contention would soon swirl, whose probing, sensual, and erotic vision tested the limits of what many thought could constitute art. That both artists would die within a few years of this photograph gives this encounter a charged poignancy.

Warhol stares straight at the camera, his endlessly malleable and chameleon-like face reminiscent of some forlorn waif out of a painting by Antoine Watteau. His gaze is vulnerability personified, touching and wondrous in its accessibility. The eyes that probed the constructs and directions of American culture look out in trusting blankness, fixing us with an almost mesmerizing quality. To the many who saw Warhol as the consummate charlatan, his visage here becomes one more evasive mask, just another fictive pose by the ultimate poseur. To those who read him as the discoverer of unexpected and surprising truths, though, the emotion Mapplethorpe captures by quite straightforward means is yet one more revelation of this curious master. In either case, the fundamental ambiguities that have come to define Warhol remain secure; his blankness must always be filled by his viewers.

Mapplethorpe's manipulations of the setting of this photograph make his reading of Warhol's significance fairly clear. By posing Warhol against a bare but spotlit wall, he surrounds his subject with a kind of halo: Warhol becomes the light that illuminates the darkness, the long-suffering mystic and modern saint in ill-fitting wig who can expiate our sins. It is perhaps significant that both artists were Catholic; Mapplethorpe, in any case, understood the function and force of an icon, and in placing Warhol in a redemptive relation to us he treads on interesting ground. (For another version of this photograph, Mapplethorpe constructed a frame in the shape of a cross.) He presents Warhol to us as the possessor of a special and holy power, and suggests the possibility that this stature was not achieved without personal cost. JY

46
Andy Warhol, 1986
Photograph, ed. 5/10
27 1/2 x 24 1/4

Robert Mapplethorpe,
born Floral Park, New York,
1946; died in Boston, 1989

Brice **Marden**

47
Couplet Painting Study III, 1987-88
Ink on paper
22 x 10 1/4

Brice Marden, born Bronxville, New York, 1938; lives in New York City

Brice Marden's recent paintings and drawings came as a bit of a shock to the art world when they were first exhibited in the mid 1980s. Here, after all, was an artist whose work for two decades had helped define the minimalist aesthetic. Those elegant and severe multi-paneled paintings, so judicious and refined, seemed remarkable episodes of control and reason. Marden's earlier paintings were seductive abstract and geometric juxtapositions, tone poems realized in the very subtlest colors, liberation achieved through pensive restraint.

But what then of works such as *Couplet Painting Study III*? Nothing appears planned or logical; instead, here is pictorial frenzy, a spider web of mania that seems to erupt from the heart rather than the mind. Ink lines swim across its surface with dizzying aplomb. Raging and willful calligraphic slashes churn their way across Marden's surface, cascading like some Oriental landscape, restless and probing, willing to sacrifice harmony for expression. If this is Marden's voice in 1988, can it be reconciled with his earlier work, or is it instead a negation of his previous vision?

It could be argued that *Couplet Painting Study III* stays well within Marden's overall artistic pursuits, and, though in a surprising idiom, stands for the same things his art always has. Although his earlier works appeared resolved and sedate, they only did so after long and arduous processes of addition and subtraction. Marden's endless fussing and experimentations with tremendously subtle calibrations of shape, color, and tone were completely subsumed in the impassive appearances of the final artwork. But they were there, bubbling just beneath the surface, and his recent work is their rampant confession. Now Marden's activities do not conceal one another, their temporal presence obscured and modified by subsequent events. Instead, every moment retains its memory, exhibiting the immediate evidence of Marden's hand. A state of flux replaces a state of resolve, but reached through similar processes of inquiry. Both modes of Marden's art betray the workings of a mind determined to bring his surfaces a kind of solution. In a curious way, neither his ends nor his means have changed all that much. JY

Agnes **Martin**

The abstract art of our century has been beset by contradictory impulses. On one hand, visionaries like Piet Mondrian or Jackson Pollock attempted to bypass the distracting minutiae of the visible world, providing access to the hidden essence of things. On the other, more down-to-earth types like Donald Judd and Frank Stella discounted the possibility of the spiritual plane. Instead, they insisted, in Stella's words, that "what you see is what you see," and that an art object should not pretend to be anything more than the pure mute matter of which it is made.

The great paradox of Agnes Martin's work is that her paintings share the aspirations of the first group and the visual vocabulary of the second. Her trademark is the grid, lightly drawn with thin pencil lines and overlaid with simple bands of subtly shaded grays and whites. In *Untitled II,* she eliminates the grid's vertical component, leaving just a field of horizontal lines that divide the canvas like a sheet of ruled paper. Nothing, it seems, could be more straightforward, nothing more obviously "there."

Yet something about this painting defies easy categorization. Simple as it is, it contains almost imperceptible irregularities and variations that suggest deeper intentions. For instance, the pencil lines are obviously hand drawn, wavering ever so slightly as they stretch across the canvas in a way that reminds us of the human presence behind these works. The variations of gray and white are at times so close in tone that they almost merge. From a distance, the surface seems luminous, implying that behind the paint is not just a piece of stretched canvas, but an inaccessible world of shimmering atmosphere. In Martin's hands, geometry is not static, but trembles with incipient life.

"My interest is in experience that is wordless and silent," Martin explained to Thomas McEvilley in *Artforum* in 1987, "and [in] the fact that this experience can be expressed for me in art work which is also wordless and silent." Though her work first achieved prominence in the early 1960s during the birth of the minimalist movement, Martin was born the same year as Pollock, the legendary Abstract Expressionist. In paintings that are as restrained as Pollock's are extroverted, Martin nevertheless shares with her contemporary a yearning to make art that touches the otherwise unreachable corners of the human soul. EH

48
Untitled II, 1988
Acrylic, pencil on canvas
72 x 72

Agnes Martin, born Maklin, Saskatchewan, 1912;
lives in Santa Fe

Allan **McCollum**

From the corner of the eye, there is nothing particularly unusual about a display of Allan McCollum's *Surrogates*, an arrangement of small framed pictures hung a bit haphazardly on the wall. It is only when one focuses full attention on this grouping that things begin to seem strange. At the center of each of these tidy frames is a flat black rectangle. Where, one wonders, is the art? What has happened to the photograph or drawing that ought to appear inside the frame? Further peculiarities arise. On close examination, it becomes clear that these are not framed pictures at all, but solid cast objects painted in shades of black, gray, and white. What is going on here?

The author of these paradoxes is an artist whose career has consisted of a series of guerilla attacks on some of our culture's more cherished illusions about art. The primary target of McCollum's *Surrogates* is the notion of the preciousness of art—the idea that an art object is special and unique and belongs to an entirely different category than the mass-produced items that litter department store shelves. McCollum argues that there is no real difference between art and other high-priced consumer goods. He proves his point by eliminating all the "art" from these art objects and then sending them out into the art market to be displayed, bought, and sold like any other painting or sculpture.

McCollum's project is not so much to destroy the concept of art as to bring it back down to earth. He reminds us that, when auction prices for old-master paintings are front-page news and successful artists aspire to Hollywood-style celebrity, it is simply wishful thinking to imagine that art is somehow not of this world. In other bodies of work, McCollum approaches this issue from alternate directions. His *Perfect Vehicles* (1986-) for instance, are groups of solid cast forms, identical in shape but varying in color, which mimic the look of decorator vases. Here he zeroes in on the marketing of art—the way in which the myth that every art object is unique is used to create an illusion of choice among what are essentially interchangeable objects.

Like many other artists who gained prominence in the 1980s, McCollum maintains an ambivalent attitude toward the commercialization of art which was the hallmark of that decade. He subtly undermines the tendency to equate commercial and aesthetic value by carrying it to absurdity. At the same time, he places his *Surrogate* paintings inside the very marketing system they criticize. In the process, he challenges the viewer to consider his or her own complicity in a process that reduces art to just another luxury item. EH

49
Surrogates, 1983
Cast hydrocal, enamel paint; twenty units variable dimensions

Allan McCollum, born Los Angeles, 1944; lives in New York City

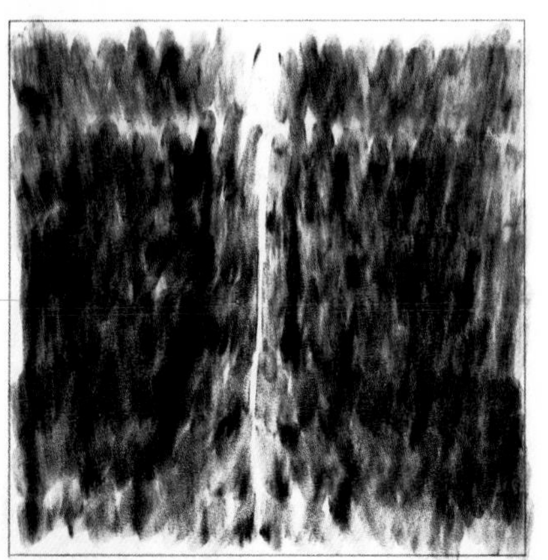

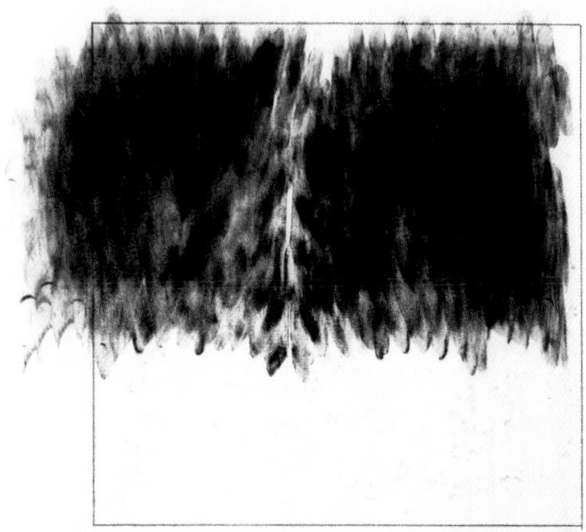

Robert **Morris**

Several times over the course of his career—in 1973, 1976, and 1985 to be exact—Robert Morris has made drawings in an ongoing series called *Blind Time.* The project has afforded Morris the opportunity to inquire into several specific aspects of the processes of art making. In this drawing, he is particularly interested in investigating strictures of time, aesthetic possibilities that might be uncovered during sense deprivation, and discipline enforced within a structured and predetermined activity.

The legend that appears at the lower left of *Untitled* is the key to Morris's activity. On a large prepared sheet of paper, Morris has drawn two squares. In the left-hand square, he dutifully enacted the ritual described in the legend: with his fingers smeared with graphite, Morris made short up and down strokes every second for a minute, attempting to fill in the square. The square, with its six hundred mini-strokes across the surface, is not fully covered with graphite; one minute was insufficient to complete the task, particularly since Morris used all ten fingers in tandem, rather than directing them toward chosen areas. The square retains a distinct left and right bipartite articulation, as the physical structure of Morris's arms kept his hands each to one side. But the square is no failure; Morris's interest is not to create a finished drawing, but to record a temporal event. The drawing is a residue, the extant result of a performance activity.

In the right square, it's "blind time." With his eyes closed, holding his breath, counting seconds, Morris attempted to duplicate the effort he had just concluded at the left, but with markedly different results. His hands now move to and fro in a different discipline, leaving large areas of the square blank, and straying outside its boundaries. A record of manual rather than visual activity, the right square is an experiment into what happens when an artist is denied sight, the sense thought to be at the very core of his or her talent. (In parts of the 1976 series, Morris, fascinated by the possibilities of a mind totally free of pictorial suggestion, collaborated with a woman who had been blind since birth.) By introducing new rules into art making, Morris brings its component processes into analysis. In abjuring and sacrificing some of his abilities, he exposes their own dictates and principles. Morris has been blind, and now can see. JY

50
Untitled, 1973
Graphite on paper
35 x 46

Robert Morris, born Kansas City, Missouri, 1931; lives in New York City

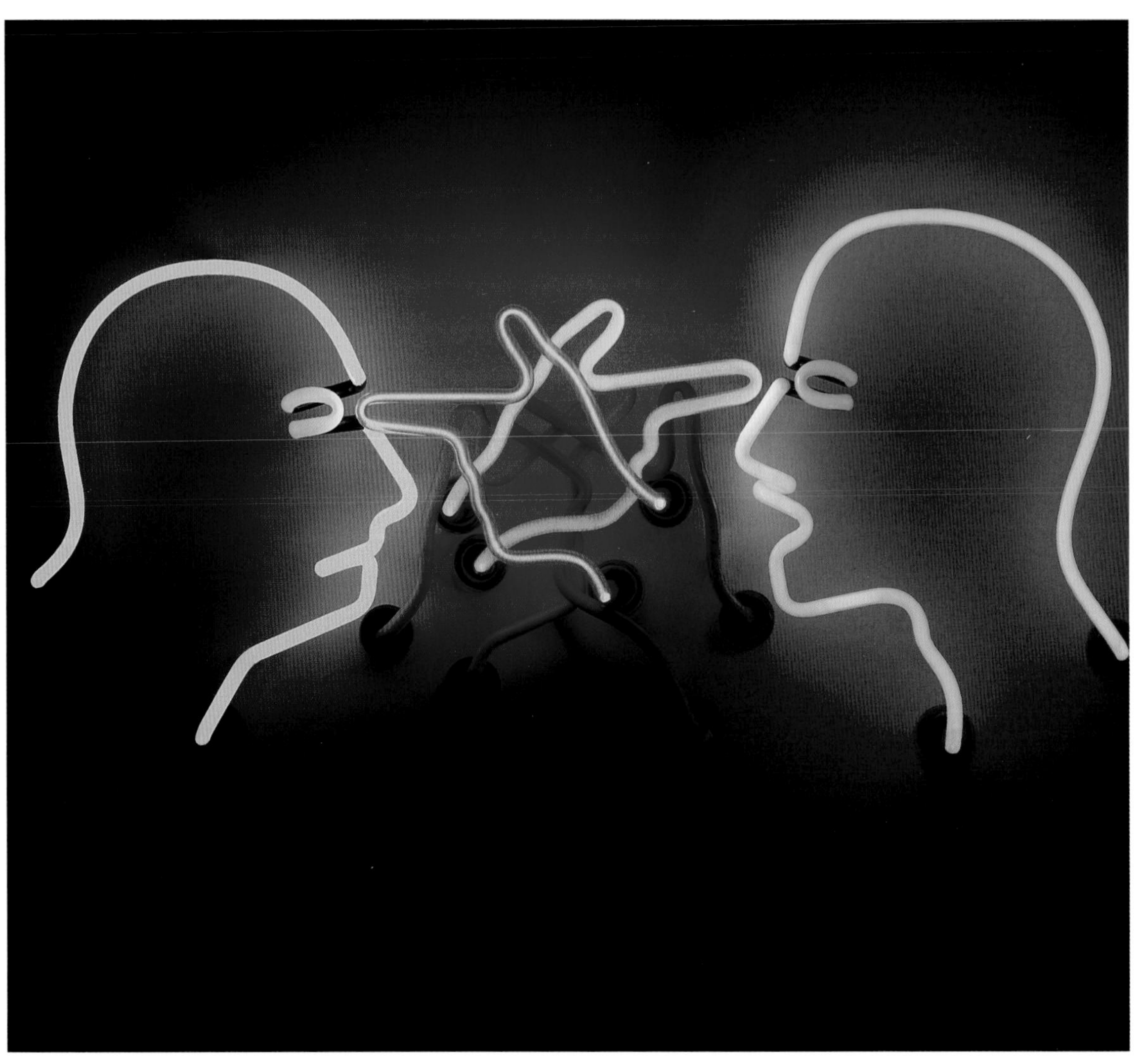

Bruce **Nauman**

51
Double Poke in the Eye II, 1985
Neon, aluminum, ed. 13/40
24 x 36 x 6 1/4

Bruce Nauman, born Fort Wayne, Indiana, 1941; lives in Pecos, New Mexico

Since the 1960s, Bruce Nauman has made art out of sandstone, fiberglass, neon, wood, aluminum, rope, wax, plaster, fluorescent light, mirrors, wallboard, foam rubber, felt, steel, and masking tape, in addition to an ambitious body of work in video and film, poetry, prints, and drawings. No single thread or artistic aspiration can unite all the various aspects of his vision, but there is running through Nauman's work a persistent inquiry and challenge as to how language—both visual and literary—works, and how systems of communication may reveal their machinations when turned in on themselves, often with a razor-sharp sense of humor.

Nauman is one of a group of talented artists, including Robert Arneson and John Baldessari, who emerged in California in the 1960s. Their work is marked by a kind of mysterious accessibility, not exactly akin to the direct and instantly readable style of New York Pop, but still using recognizable cultural language in elusive and dramatic ways. On one level, *Double Poke in the Eye II* shares some characteristics with the work of Dan Flavin; both artists take advantage of the ambient nature of light. But Nauman literally bends that light to another purpose. By forming two confronting heads and, through a timing mechanism, rapidly gesticulating hands, Nauman's neon takes on narrative dimensions. Nauman knows our delight in light, especially blinking light: like kids gazing at a pinball machine or adults loose in Las Vegas, we can be mesmerized by the candy colors and staggered on-off timing of the illumination, which absorbs our attention as paint or stone would not.

Double Poke in the Eye II, like one of the sixteenth-century moralizing paintings by Hieronymus Bosch or Pieter Bruegel, bears a message beneath its veneer of humor and ease of access. In the social world, dialogue can quickly lead to argumentation, discourse can give way to threats and violence. Almost innate in our dual role as individuals and members of a group is our historical predilection toward confrontation; to be what we are as individuals almost by definition puts us in conflict with others. That the vocabulary of Nauman's contentious encounter is surprisingly similar to the actions of commodity traders gesticulating in the pits gives its presence in the Refco Collection a special and completely delightful irony.
JY

MEN

Blinky **Palermo**

In his work and in his life, the German artist Blinky Palermo, who died in 1977 at the age of thirty-four, was devoted to the notion of an art that intermingles with the world. In his quest to blur distinctions between the two realms, he went so far as to reinvent himself, literally, by adopting as an art-world alias the name of a Sicilian boxing promoter.

Palermo's conviction that art is life has its roots in early twentieth-century movements that were devoted to the utopian dream of refashioning society through art. For Palermo, this conviction was strengthened by his relationship with the late Joseph Beuys, the great artist and mystic who looms over contemporary German art as Andy Warhol does over recent art in the United States. But while Beuys was prone to flamboyant "actions" (spending a week in a cage with a coyote to demonstrate his solidarity with Native Americans, for instance), public lectures, and performances in which he acted out his philosophy, Palermo was by nature more introspective. Eschewing the public role, he focused instead on the creation of paradoxical works that subverted the traditions of modern art or subtly transformed the architectural setting in which they were placed.

Blue Triangle illustrates his approach. The notion of a painting consisting only of a bright blue triangle seems something of a joke, so simple and banal as to be almost meaningless. And yet, when doubled and arranged in a real-world setting, the triangle begins to lay claim to the space in which it is installed: suddenly an anonymous hallway is pulled into the realm of art. In this and other works, Palermo is less interested in the work of art itself than in its environment and the interaction between the two. A similar message pervades a series of cloth paintings stitched together from commercial fabrics. From a distance, they deceptively suggest conventional color-field paintings. Only up close does their status as humble yard goods become evident, effectively puncturing the expectations of an audience seeking an "art experience" removed from the banalities of everyday life.

Despite the brevity of his life, Palermo has been an important influence not only on younger German artists such as Günther Förg and Reinhard Mucha, but also on American artists, including Peter Halley and Sherrie Levine, exploring a kind of generic abstraction whose meanings must be located in the world beyond the canvas. Still, Palermo remains something of an enigma. The quiet hermeticism of his work only unlocks itself for the viewer willing to look beyond the obvious. Forceful and paradoxical, his paintings suggest the fallacies inherent in any vision that would set art apart as an idealized, isolated realm of experience. EH

52
Blue Triangle, 1969
Original drawing with handpainting, cardboard stencil, paint tube, brush, cardboard box, ed. 24/50
variable dimensions

Blinky Palermo, born Leipzig, Germany, 1943; died in Malé, Maldive Islands, 1977

Giulio **Paolini**

53
Intervallo, 1974
Plaster; two units
each 38 1/2 x 21 x 4

Giulio Paolini, born Genoa, Italy, 1940; lives in Turin

Associated with the Italian movement known as *Arte Povera*, or Poor Art, which emerged in the late 1960s, Guilio Paolini shares this group's distrust in the principles of reason and progress. However, while his colleagues by and large have reacted against the dehumanizing quality of modern industrial life with a celebration of history and the generative powers of nature, Paolini has chosen instead to expose the false promises of art. Incorporating in his work plaster casts of antique sculpture, copies of sixteenth- and seventeenth-century engravings, fragments of Corinthian columns, and optical diagrams of the sort that fascinated Renaissance scholars, he borrows from the vocabulary of classical Greek and Italian Renaissance art. Constantly throwing our attention back on these two historical moments, he reminds us of our tendency to see them as golden ages of Western civilization, periods when the joint forces of art and science seemed poised to master the world.

However, instead of affirming this confidence, Paolini uses these traditions to express the uncertain sensibility of our far more troubled time. In *Intervallo*, for instance, he splits a replica of a twisted classical torso in two, and installs each half against a facing wall. Suddenly the magnificent perfection and purity of the classical sculpture is lost; it becomes a fragmented form, struggling on one side to free itself from the blank matter represented by the wall and on the other to lose itself in the void from which it sprang. In its disunity, this work might stand for the confused and divided soul of modern man.

Paolini has made similar points in other works. In his hands, the perspective diagram, used by Renaissance artists to create a convincing simulacrum of the visible world, becomes an arbitrary system of representation, an illusion in actuality no more "real" than those systems used by medieval, Asian, or modern artists. He is also interested in photography for its ability to reinvent the world and to multiply the realities before us. Thus, despite their apparent clarity and analytic precision, Paolini's works are in fact tantalizingly enigmatic. We sense that there are mysteries behind them which the tools of science and philosophy cannot begin to penetrate. Reason, Paolini seems to be telling us, is simply another game we play to hold off the chaos beyond. EH

A. R. **Penck**

Though not quite akin to the ride of the Valkyries, the onslaught of German artists such as Georg Baselitz, Walter Dahn, Jörg Immendorff, Anselm Kiefer, A. R. Penck, Sigmar Polke, and Gerhard Richter overwhelmed the art world of the 1980s. Bringing boldness, aggressive energy, and, for the most part, a determined interest in figuration, this extraordinary blitz of talent changed the course of art history, as the work of these artists came to define the parameters of the movement known as Neo-Expressionism. Bluster and panache was the order of the day, bursting through chaotic surfaces of gesture and color, all charged up at frantic speeds.

But they had an impish masquerader in their midst. There is really no such artist as A. R. Penck; the name of the nineteenth-century scientist famous for studies of the geomorphology of the glacial epoch is a pseudonym employed by Ralf Winkler, a frenetic painter who left East Germany for Cologne in 1980. Under this alias—Winkler has used others, too, calling himself on occasion Tancred Mitchell, Alpha, Ypsilon, and even Mike Hammer—he has created some of the most inventive pictures of our time. Completely self-taught and somewhat suppressed as an artist while living in the East, Penck nevertheless managed to develop his own brash and personal artistic vocabulary.

Untitled reads like a hieroglyphic run amok. A warrior stick figure, abstract symbols, decorated heads, a snake, house, and two imposing gyrating figures populate its surface, jumbled together as if in some strange narrative, in a ritual whose exact meaning is unclear. Penck's attitude toward his materials implies a sense of urgency; *Untitled* appears to have been rapidly slathered in black paint over an untreated, mundane, brown corrugated cardboard surface. Ideas flow seemingly unmediated and unrelated, stubbornly filling every bit of space yet not overlapping. Their accretion gives the impression of a primal outpouring, not too dissimilar from prehistoric cave painting, aboriginal art, or early Greek vase painting. And like those forms of expression, *Untitled* has a canny ring of truth about it. In his fury of mark-making, what Penck reveals can suggest something more direct and important than what expert technical craft could expose. We might not be able to "read" this image, but its almost psychic weight makes us suspect that it may illustrate a text or a cosmology we have temporarily forgotten. JY

54
Untitled, 1982
Oil on cardboard
70 3/4 x 90 1/2

A. R. Penck, born Dresden, 1939; lives in Cologne

Sylvia **Plimack-Mangold**

Art history textbooks identify the Hudson River School as an important movement in nineteenth-century American landscape painting. Its goals included not only describing the broad open spaces then to be found in upstate New York, but also somehow conveying the spirituality sensed in those places, the notion that a benevolent Creator had made the Catskill Mountains a special and gentle locale. Artists such as Asher B. Durand and Thomas Cole chronicled the glories of the Hudson River valley, where a new nation counted its divine blessings.

Sylvia Plimack-Mangold has lived in upstate New York since 1971, and paintings like *Winterset* are her responses to the still vivid poetry of nature and site. Her earlier work was marked by a focused and almost claustrophobic photorealism. Paintings of bare hardwood floors and corners of empty rooms were scrupulous records of specific places, dry and studied examinations of space and form. In those paintings, Plimack-Mangold mastered the technique of having paint totally dissemble its own nature, becoming, in true *trompe l'oeil* manner, the exact simulation of the stuff it described. Her pictures of floors and walls were almost obsessive in their palpability.

Plimack-Mangold's extended residence in the foothills of the Catskills eventually led her to raise her sights from the floor to her windows, through which she beheld a panoply of nature. By 1977, the misty moors of her environs began to play a larger and larger role in her work, and in rendering these luminous spaces she has departed from her effort toward verisimilitude. She is sensitive to the unending nuances surrounding her, to the magical fusions of tone and atmosphere each hour and observation can bring. Plimack-Mangold transfers these subtleties to canvas through the application of broad areas of color. In *Winterset,* her paint shimmers and flows across the linen surface to show a black and moribund earth sleeping beneath a dreamy sky of lavender and pink.

But Plimack-Mangold has not completely abjured her interest in realism; she retains an element reminding us of the ambiguous differences between the depicted and the real. On three sides of *Winterset*, Plimack-Mangold applies oil paint in an astounding duplication of masking tape. The sublime meets the mundane, nature abuts artifice, all brought into being by the vision and expertise of an artist. It seems crucial to Plimack-Mangold to balance these worlds, to juxtapose what can be seen with what can be felt. The intervals are interesting places. JY

55
Winterset, 1981
Oil on canvas
60 x 80

Sylvia Plimack-Mangold, born New York City, 1938; lives in Washingtonville, New York

Sigmar **Polke**

The Near East has fired the imagination of Western culture for more than a thousand years. Rumors of Islamic splendor helped provoke the Great Crusades, and in more recent times personages from the Sheik of Araby to King Tut, Lawrence of Arabia, and Omar Khayyam have intrigued the European mind. The Levant seemed a world of wonder, of harem girls and desert tribes, heady spices and deep mystery. In art, the escapism the Arab world offered Europe was compelling, and many artists—notably J. A. D. Ingres, Eugène Delacroix, and Henri Matisse—practiced a kind of Orientalism where Western desires and fantasies were extended and fulfilled. It doesn't matter much that these artists' presentation of the Islamic world was a fiction; what was important was the outlet that fiction allowed.

Orientalism makes a comeback in Sigmar Polke's *Untitled*. Prominent among German artists who led a return to pointed cultural inquiry in the 1960s and seventies, Polke has often utilized pre-existing photographs, altering them to serve his needs. He embellishes the surface of *Untitled*, applying tempera paint in a way that almost turns this into a hand-colored photograph. Polke augments certain areas, and then dabs on paint in random patterns that create a decorative effect. His intervention is everywhere evident, but it does no more than garnish this photograph and assert his presence.

Written beneath the artist's signature at the bottom right of *Untitled* is "Qetta 1974," alluding to the source of this photo. Qetta is the name of both a town in Afghanistan, and a smallish city in Pakistan, and Polke must have visited one of these places that year. (The artist is in the photograph, at the far right, his eyeglasses emphasized by overpaint.) Four years later, Polke had the photo enlarged, and turned it into *Untitled*. The image is a transformed memory, a recollection of peripheral involvement in an alien culture. It has the pungent smell of the hookah, the sense of an indolence without beginning or end, a melancholy that is palpable, and—a European witness, his garb and body language bespeaking his foreignness and status as voyeur. Polke's search for meaning and content, his desire to find something that might be important or carry weight, makes him ready to appropriate the rhythms of another culture. Through *Untitled*, he can admire, do homage, recognize, but he cannot participate. JY

56
Untitled, 1978
Egg tempera on black-and-white photograph
24 1/2 x 36 1/2

Sigmar Polke, born Oels, Germany [now Olesnica, Poland], 1941; lives in Hamburg and Cologne

Richard **Prince**

Like a number of other artists of his generation, Richard Prince is simultaneously fascinated by and skeptical of the "truths" promulgated by magazines, television, advertising, and movies. In his art, he acts like an archaeologist from some distant future, piecing together an image of our culture from a scrap pile which consists, not of pottery shards or architectural ruins, but of the fragmented media images and slogans that daily bombard us with relentless intensity. Prince's raw materials include such diverse stuff as magazine ads, Playboy cartoons, strippers' publicity photographs, and Superman comics. One body of work was based on the macho Marlboro Man, while another focused on "biker chicks," snapshots of girlfriends sent in for publication by the readers of motorcycle magazines. Prince simply rephotographs these images and presents them without comment, either in their entirety, or as telling details. Thus removed from their ordinary setting into an art context, they become strange and unnatural, and we begin to realize the extent to which our vision of the world is colored by the persuasive fictions of the media.

Prince is an heir to Pop art, but while artists like Andy Warhol and James Rosenquist celebrated the aura of glamour and excitement that surrounds popular culture, Prince is far more suspicious. He takes us behind the scenes, as it were, to reveal the artifice behind the illusion. When he rephotographs the Marlboro Man, for instance, he crops the images to focus on details like hand gestures or clothing, then enlarges them until they become grainy and hard to read. In the process, the authenticity of this rugged icon is somehow tarnished and we realize that this image is more indebted to movies than to any historical reality.

In *Waves, Bangs, Palms*, Prince presents what he refers to as a "gang" of images lifted without alteration from surfing and lifestyle magazines. The almost identical configurations of these apparently disparate objects—a breaking wave, a fringe of hair, and a palm leaf—reveal that these items are for all practical purposes interchangeable symbols for the good life. Each in its own way has become a kind of shorthand for the leisure-time pursuit of pleasure. By isolating these images and displaying them on a single sheet of paper like a collection of laboratory specimens, Prince encourages us to take a far more dispassionate look than usual at the way even our most private fantasies and desires can be manufactured and manipulated. EH

57
Waves, Bangs, Palms, 1987
Ektacolor photograph
86 x 47

Richard Prince, born Panama Canal Zone, 1949; lives in New York City

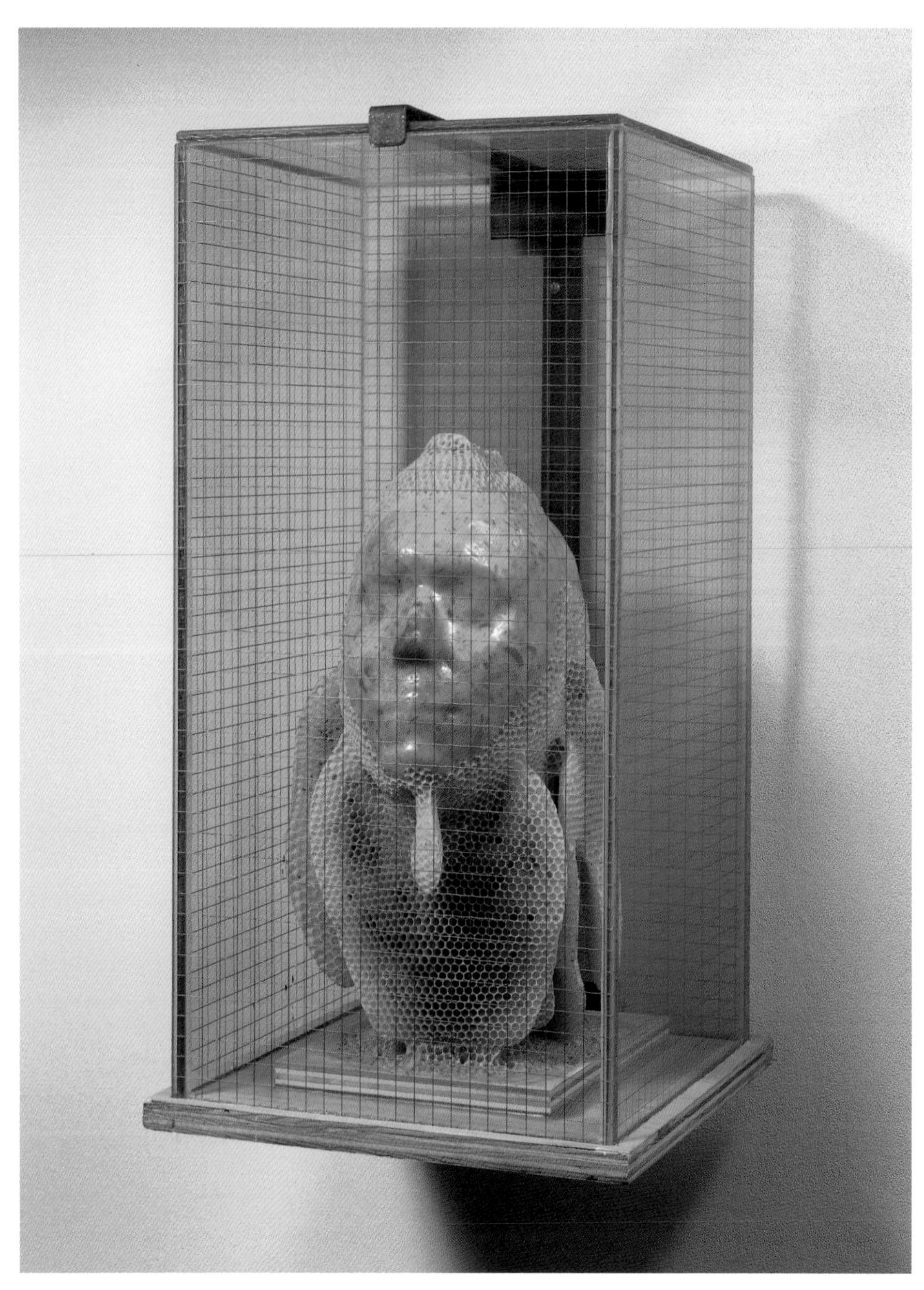

Garnett **Puett**

"Pluralism" was one of the terms used to characterize the art of the 1980s, a decade that appeared to have no dominant style but exhibited instead widely disparate artistic aims. Modern art, it seemed, had become a grab bag of experiments and possibilities resisting simple categorization; many artists were exploring completely new avenues of art making. Such an investigator and pioneer is Garnett Puett, who makes art with bees. For *EM II*, Puett built a steel armature of a male head and covered it with beeswax. He then encased the object in glass, installed a queen bee in a notched recess still visible at the top of the sculpture, covered certain areas he wanted developed (beard and hair) with a sticky substance, and introduced several thousand bees. The bees proceeded to follow the dictates of their nature; they used the sticky areas as a base for their work, and industriously set about honeycombing layer after layer in beautiful hexagonal patterns. When the sculpture reached his perception of completion, Puett removed the bees with a vacuum cleaner, took out the honey, cleaned the surface of the piece, froze it to kill any larvae, and resealed it in its glass case.

Puett's is a kind of unwitting art, with bees exploited not for their honey but for their sense of order, instinctual urge toward symmetry, communal discipline, and single-minded pursuit of a goal. The artist also senses our deep-seated fear of bees, and it is frightening to imagine the surging masses of bees, wave after wave of them furiously covering this face. But Puett's process is by no means mere gimmickry; more than bees are at work here. Puett imbues *EM II* with a moody resonance, impassive gaze, and stoic resignation that gives this figure the air of some Egyptian pharaoh, staring out of his vitrine for all eternity. Puett's family runs one of the biggest honey-producing firms in America, and he studied entomology in college before becoming an artist. He brings to his art that experience and understanding, but extends it into the creation of objects that are successful not because of how they were made, but because of the power that results from his unusual inquiry. JY

58
EM II, 1987
Wax, steel, wood, glass case
24 3/4 x 13 x 13

Garnett Puett, born
Hahira, Georgia, 1959;
lives in Brooklyn, New York

Martin **Puryear**

Consummate design, scrupulous craftsmanship, nuanced abstraction, and a myriad of interdependent balances can all be found in the sculptures of Martin Puryear. A piece such as *Endgame* seems completely composed of what are usually seen as opposites: it is sculpture and painting, delicate and strong, organic and geometric, finished and raw, open and closed, tense and reconciled, linear and volumetric, accessible and removed, direct and ambiguous. Its profile on the wall seems quite elementary—a painted pipe of pine coiled toward forming a circle. One end is open, its edge painted a dusty yellow, its interior a wispy blue green. The other end is capped with a lavender seal rimmed in reddish orange. The rest of *Endgame*'s exterior is painted a grayish black.

This striking shape is a compendium of suggestions, achieved through Puryear's concentration and control. It is, of course, no pipe of pine; such a thing could not have the shape or silhouette we see here. Wood—and, by extension, nature—is here bent to new purposes, manipulated to reveal rhythms it would not except for the artist's intervention. A careful examination of the open end of *Endgame* shows it to be made up of no fewer than thirty separate pieces of wood painstakingly joined and laminated together. *Endgame's* broad curve is composed of a variety of smaller actions, an almost obsessive annealing. Each strip of pine is subjected to the good of the whole, runs its course under Puryear's command, and adheres to its neighbor in a spirited teamwork.

This is woodworking raised to high art, and salient aspects of Puryear's training brought him these special skills. While a Peace Corps volunteer in Sierra Leone, he became sensitive to the possibilities of natural materials and to the harmonies inherent in bold and seemingly simple shapes. His later studies at the Swedish Royal Academy of Art in Stockholm exposed him to the traditions of modern Scandinavian furniture design, with its sophisticated principles of wood joinery. But Puryear's art is not formed by any collection of influences; rather, it is the end to which these means are aimed that is of interest. Puryear's achievement is to create moody and reserved objects that seem to pulse with unanswerable and surprising questions. He shows how difficult it can be to make simple things, and how simple things can be very difficult. JY

59
Endgame, 1985
Painted pine
65 x 62 x 3 3/4

Martin Puryear, born Washington, D.C., 1941; lives in Accord, New York

Holt **Quentel**

Holt Quentel's frayed and battered paintings have the look of old tarps left out in the rain too many times. Or perhaps, given the once crisp geometric motifs, letters, or numbers emblazoned across their faded surfaces, we may see them as fragments of military banners or flags whose bold insignia have fallen victim to the vagaries of time and neglect. In fact, however, the deteriorated state of these works has been carefully and painstakingly manufactured. Quentel makes these paintings by stitching together fragments of raw, unstretched canvas, painting over them, assaulting them with an electric sander, softening them in a washer and dryer, and leaving them in a crumpled pile to fade for days in her studio. In a gesture calculated to confound the preciousness of art, she equips each painting with a canvas duffle bag into which it may be slipped between installations.

Despite its apparent simplicity, a work like *Green Cross* conveys a mix of messages. On one level, it offers sly commentary on America's impatience toward the past. Like the pre-aged blue jeans they at times resemble, Quentel's paintings speak of a culture that does not always distinguish between authentic and newly minted history. On another level, Quentel directs our attention to the now somewhat tarnished aspirations of modern art. The simple geometry of her paintings, the use of single letters, numbers or, as here, crosses, as primary design elements link these works to the reductive aesthetic of such modern masters as Ellsworth Kelly and early Frank Stella. But while the works of those artists contain at least a remnant of confidence in the possibility of clarity, order, and progress, Quentel offers us modernist compositions that seem literally ghosts of their former selves. Like the canvases themselves, the modernist dream seems frayed and irreparably damaged.

In a similar vein, these paintings mock as well the pretensions of the ideals of statehood and empire, whose flags they resemble. Ripped to ribbons, they imply the bitter realities behind the fantasy of glory which, throughout the centuries, has driven so many young men to their deaths. In the end, Quentel's patchwork paintings reflect back on the traditions of modern art while they simultaneously face outward to the world beyond. They suggest the ways in which history is remade and utopian visions exploited in the struggle to define a society's goals. Tattered monuments to lost dreams, these battered cloths are imbued with ambivalence, as they point at once toward the possibilities of hope and the dangers of freedom. EH

60
Green Cross, 1989
Latex, canvas, rope
84 x 84

Holt Quentel, born
Milwaukee, 1961;
lives in New York City

Arnulf **Rainer**

The work of Arnulf Rainer picks up the thread of Modernism that leads back to Abstract Expressionism, Surrealism, and German Expressionism. His performances and painted photographs explore the workings of the psyche under stress, peeling back the behavior patterns imposed by social convention to reveal intense emotional states that lurk just below the surface. Significantly, Rainer is a native of Vienna, which was also home to Sigmund Freud. Like his countryman, Rainer is fascinated with the demons of the unconscious. Much of his work revolves around the self-portrait, employed as an instrument of self-discovery. His *Face Farces* and *Body Language/Motor Poses* begin as photographs of the artist in extreme states ranging from fear, disgust, and sorrow to rage and manic hilarity. In these photographs, Rainer assumes a parade of alter egos—at times shaving his hair, wearing disguises, removing his clothes, even undergoing apparent gender shifts—thereby suggesting the fluidity of identity when the shackles of social restraint are removed.

However, these black-and-white images merely serve as raw materials over which the artist lays slashing marks and paint strokes which may all but obliterate the underlying image. Yet the traces of the photographic image, breaking through the forest of agitated marks, become all the more powerful as they hover at the brink of disintegration. Rainer explained to David Courtney of *Arts Magazine* in 1986 that "photography alone...is not able to communicate adequately a moving or statically concentrated tension." Thus, "on the paper, only a dull reflection remains." His alterations imbue these static images with a raw expressive energy and suggest that the creation of a new self must be preceded by the annihilation of the old.

Rainer has been a lifelong student of mysticism and Eastern philosophies. He is drawn as well to art historical figures like Egon Schiele and Vincent van Gogh whose paintings flirt with madness. In a kind of psychic identification, he has on occasion painted over photographs of their work. This quest to stretch the limits of mind and body, even at the risk of psychological dissolution, is a recurring theme in modern art. It is the underside of the faith in progress, revealing the hidden costs and little daily deaths involved in the drive to rationalize human behavior. The realm in which Rainer immerses himself is one most of us strive to avoid, but as his explosive work reminds us, we deny it at our peril. EH

61
Body Language (Körpersprache), 1971
Crayon, oil, pencil on photograph
19 3/4 x 23 1/4

Arnulf Rainer, born Baden, Austria, 1929; lives in Vienna

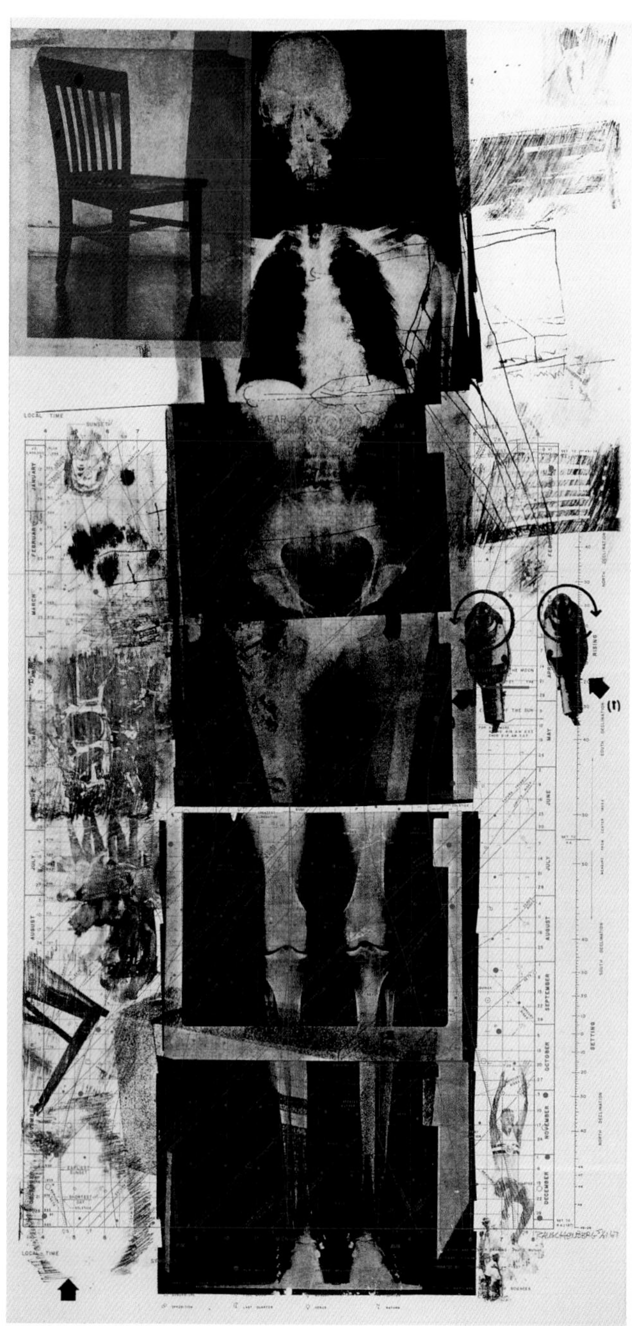

Robert **Rauschenberg**

When Robert Rauschenberg executed this lithograph and silkscreen at Gemini G.E.L. Press in Los Angeles in 1967, it was the largest image ever printed on a hand-operated lithographic press. If any single thing has defined the career of this challenging artist, it has been his unending need to probe the edges of art, exceed its constraints, test its breaking point. In *Booster*, Rauschenberg does for printmaking what he had earlier done with his "combines" for the traditions of painting and sculpture—he forces us to expand our definitions of the medium, bending its dictates to fit his requirements. As an artist, Rauschenberg has never quite behaved according to the rules; his spirit of invention has shown us the explosive and liberating freedom losing those principles can bring.

But *Booster* is, of course, a great deal more than an aesthetic rampage. Its size was dictated by Rauschenberg's desire that it carry a full-scale reproduction of a sequence of x-rays of his body. Naked in this image except for his hobnail boots, Rauschenberg presents what must be the ultimate self-portrait; we literally see inside his body, and can feel him in his bones. But despite this frankness, part of the ironic charge of *Booster* is that the x-rays in a sense conceal him: beneath our skins we all look remarkably similar, and what defines Rauschenberg's persona eludes the scan of radiation we see displayed here.

Booster undoubtedly takes its title from the way the stacked x-rays resemble the fuel stages of rockets (so much on the minds of the 1960s), an identification reinforced by the print's emphatic verticality. Rauschenberg accumulates additional visual data over the entire print. An astral chart for 1967 is superimposed over his body, again suggesting a space-age context, and giving the work a kind of time signature. A wooden chair (seen whole, and in fragments), a leaping athlete, two electric drills (strategically placed just next to the artist's groin), and echoes from other works of art all accrue around Rauschenberg's skeleton. Their appearance here does not necessarily lead to any single specific or literal meaning; Rauschenberg's art is no simple rebus to be dissected and read sequentially. In *Booster*, he brings pieces of the world together in a curious amalgam that invites a meditation on his—and by extension our—mortality. Rauschenberg's temporal shell is fully revealed to us, but his spirit must still elude our grasp. Like some latter-day Shroud of Turin, the print is finally a dazzling, spectacular, and poetic rumination on the reality and unreality of corporeality. JY

62
Booster, 1967
Lithograph, silkscreen,
ed. 37/38
72 x 36

Robert Rauschenberg, born Port Arthur, Texas, 1925; lives in New York City and Captiva Island, Florida

Richard **Rezac**

63
Untitled (Laurel Shelf), 1988
Cast bronze, wood
16 1/2 x 20 1/2 x 7 1/2

Richard Rezac, born Lincoln, Nebraska, 1952; lives in Chicago

The comparison may at first seem odious, but certain aspects of Richard Rezac's *Untitled (Laurel Shelf)* are most clearly revealed in an analysis with another sculpture in Refco's collection, Haim Steinbach's *together naturally.* In both pieces, a specially constructed shelflike pedestal supports an object or sequence of objects. Both sculptures are horizontal and adhere to a wall, and both present elements that play circular and horizontal forms against each other. The two sculptures each display some thing, but with perceivably different ends. What Steinbach presents aloofly, coyly, with irony and distance, Rezac makes with a barely concealed passion, a love of tactile substances, and a sensuous richness of touch.

Steinbach's severe pedestal, all machine-cut sharp angles and pristinely sealed with fictive formica, contrasts greatly with the ineffable poetry of Rezac's delicately stained and subtly curved wooden shelf. Rezac seems to luxuriate in the organic quality of wood, and is loathe to cover it; the carefully calculated widths and lengths of his elements, and their manner of meeting in junctures of pure harmony can be curiously breathtaking. Rezac's art is a channeling of many subtle decisions, a graceful reconciliation of elements into a lyrical whole.

And while on Steinbach's shelf lie store-bought things, a telling admission that his role is to juggle and re-present pre-existing stuff, on Rezac's shelf rests a cast bronze element, its medium a throwback to an earlier time. Three curved forms rise and fall out of a central horizontal element, the entire bronze resting on two of them. There is a tender geometry here, a swelling and then absence of form rewarding visual inspection with unexpected nuances. Rezac's bronze retains a memory of the foundry; hot fires can be reckoned beneath its cool surface. As with the respectful presentation of some Chinese bronze vessel in a museum, there is a kind of aptness and logic in the measured pace of Rezac's display. His art exhibits a belief in craft, and in the inherent dignity of art making which can be sobering to witness. While symmetry is important to Rezac, it is always imbued with a sense of touch. His achievement has been to wring a kind of abstract poetry out of the largely deafening silence of modern sculpture, and to find there something reminiscent of the presence of the human heart. JY

Gerhard **Richter**

One of the "rules" of modern art is that an artist's output should bear a recognizable "signature style." While commercial artists may be mere technicians adapting their work to patrons' whims, the argument goes, the work of a real artist will display a cohesion and unity stemming from the individual's inner self. That such rules are made to be broken is the message of Gerhard Richter, who works simultaneously in the modes of photorealism and, as in this case, abstraction.

Vivid colors sweep boldly across the canvas in *Abstract Painting 584-1*, building a dense field of jarring hues. At first glance, the scale and ambition of this work recall the creations of the Abstract Expressionists, for whom painting was a means of capturing the sublimity of nature or the agitation of private emotion. However, certain anomalies caution against this reading of Richter's work. There are, for example, the neon tones that give the painting an artificial glow. And despite the varieties of paint application (Richter may scrape, wipe, spatter, or splash paint across the canvas), we detect no sign of the artist's personal touch. Instead, the dryly mechanical surface suggests a mere parody of the gestures of self-expression. When viewed in the wider context of Richter's work, such anomalies become even more startling. His "realistic" paintings are as paradoxical as his abstractions. Drawing on traditional genres of Western art—still lifes, landscapes, and portraits—they exhibit the blurry quality of out-of-focus photographs. Instead of inviting us to admire the painter's power of illusion, a key aspect of realism, the artist insists that we recognize the artificiality of his style.

Thus, in Richter's world, nothing is what it seems. His peripatetic approach may be a response to his personal history. Having grown up in postwar Dresden and moved to West Germany just two months before the erection of the Berlin Wall, Richter is an artist suspended between two worlds, ever oscillating between the traditions of socialist realism and modernist abstraction. On the other hand, his work also relates to a more widespread sense among Western artists that modern art may have reached its limits, and that it has nothing new to say and no new way to say it. In this light, his use of multiple styles may be one way of illustrating this dilemma. However one interprets his work, Richter remains an enigma, neither willing nor able to satisfy our desire to see him safely settled into a single identity.

EH

64
Abstract Painting 584-1,
1985
Oil on canvas
69 x 98 1/2

Gerhard Richter, born
Dresden, 1932;
lives in Cologne

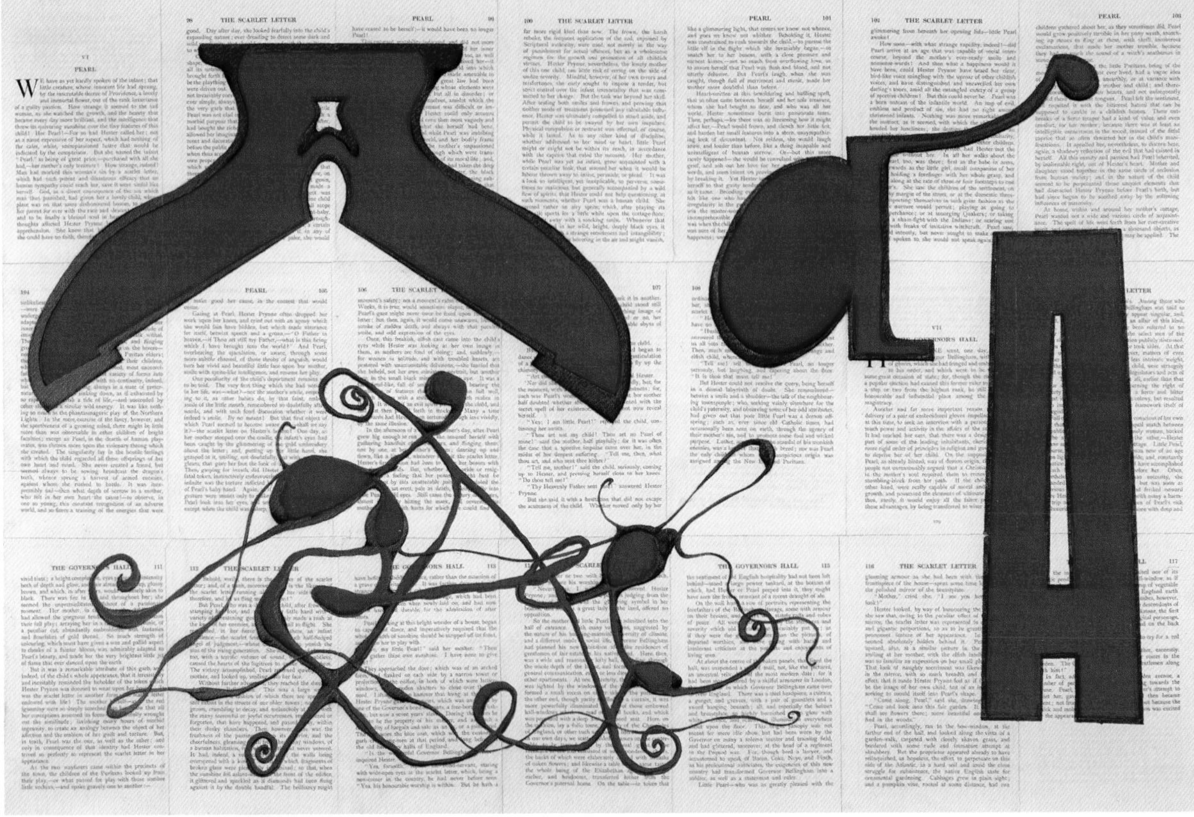

Tim **Rollins and K.O.S.**

Creativity is generally seen as an expression of unfettered individuality, transcending the constraints of social convention or group expectations. In fact, however, there is a long tradition in art, dating back to the medieval guild and the Renaissance workshop, of successful creative collaborations. Tim Rollins and the Kids of Survival constitute one of the more unusual collaborative groups working today. Rollins is a young conceptual artist whose frustration with the isolation and elitism of the art world led him to seek employment as a special education art teacher at a secondary school in New York's socially and economically troubled South Bronx. The Kids of Survival (K.O.S.) are a group of black and Hispanic high school students who work with Rollins in an after-school art program. What began ten years ago as a kind of "rap session" in which Rollins read aloud while his students doodled has evolved into a highly professional art workshop.

Each painting begins with a work of classic literature whose theme has relevance to the dilemmas of the contemporary world. K.O.S. have created paintings based, for instance, on Stephen Crane's *Red Badge of Courage,* extracting from it the idea of the pain and beauty of survival, or Franz Kafka's *America,* focusing on the joyous last chapter which offers a vision of a utopian society where everyone is an artist. Here, Nathaniel Hawthorne's *Scarlet Letter* serves as inspiration for a commentary on dignity in the face of social stigmatism.

Together, workshop members seek images to express these themes, transferring them directly onto a canvas lined with the pages of the book that served as inspiration. Rollins often directs his students' attention to art history, suggesting precedents for the imagery they have developed. When K.O.S. decided to represent *The Red Badge of Courage* with a series of wounds, he brought in images of old-master crucifixion scenes. For *The Scarlet Letter*, he introduced reproductions of the elaborately ornamented initial letters to be found in medieval illustrated manuscripts as precursors to their own scarlet A's. These art historical references, like the use of literary classics, offer the students a sense of belonging within a continuous cultural tradition. Coming at a time when many artists seem frustrated with the limitations of the art world, Rollins demonstrates that art can have meaning outside the gilded cage of gallery and museum. His workshops bring together art and life in a way that enhances both. EH

65
The Scarlet Letter–Pearl, 1986-88
Acrylic, watercolor, bistre on bookpages on linen
24 x 36

Tim Rollins, born Pittsfield, Massachusetts, 1955; lives in New York City

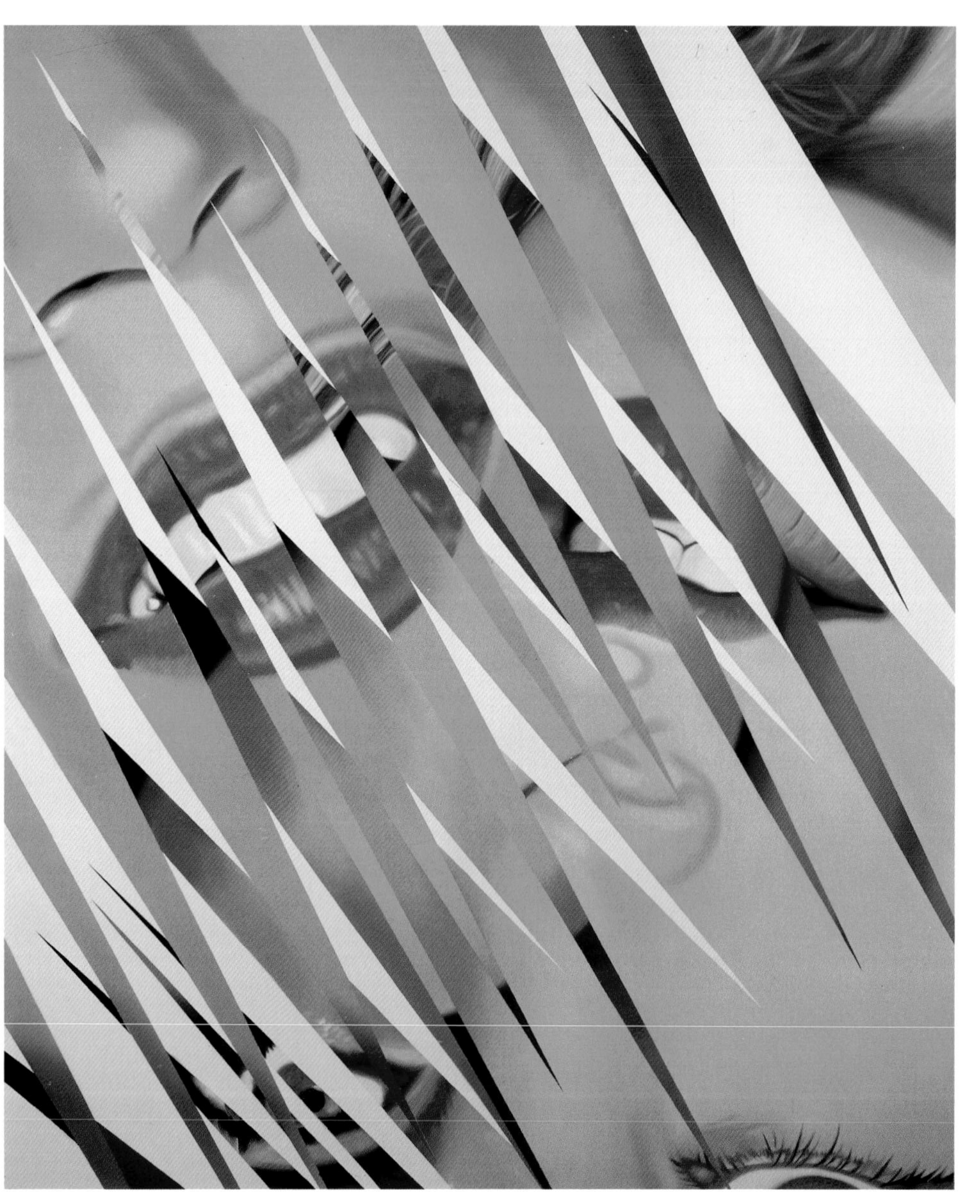

James **Rosenquist**

James Rosenquist has an assured and permanent place in the history of art. He will always be known and honored as one of the founders—along with Roy Lichtenstein, Claes Oldenburg, and Andy Warhol—of Pop art in 1960s America. Rosenquist's particular contribution was to recognize and extend into fine art the principles of popular culture and mass communication he had learned while working as a commercial billboard painter. His often immense paintings boldly juxtaposed and recombined imagery from disparate advertising sources, creating teasing and surprising pictorial assemblages that took an obvious and instantly readable language toward something that was more ambiguous, challenging, and obscure.

All four of the pop pioneers went on to have long and successful careers, and managed, more or less, to elude the stultifying status of "old master" they each would no doubt decry. Rosenquist has retained a deep interest in the possibilities of signage as social communication, in the rhetorical allure and tensions found in a clarity that is amended by pictorial editing and layering. *White Lightning* is a curious shuffle, an uneasy near-melding of two imposing female heads. Rosenquist has often utilized this image of a smiling young woman, who has come to represent for him some media-derived fantasy of Miss Model American Bombshell Consumer Adornment. She grins here (twice!) in reckless abandon, showing her clear complexion and white teeth, her redder-than-red lips parted in openness and delight.

She seems to accept her splintering deconstruction with nary a murmur nor complaint; at the core of *White Lightning* is Rosenquist's decision to razor these two heads into comblike teeth that zigzag in furious pattern. It requires a careful reading to discover, say, which nostril goes with which face, the more so since one of the heads is presented upside down. These heads are more latticed than layered, but what might seem an act of violence and savagery somewhere else is here presented as imperturbable and inevitable data. Rosenquist leaves the canvas blank at those areas where the heads do not exist or overlap, adding to our suspicion that to him these are but residues of signs, that these women are presented as artificial images, charged icons, but without personality or feeling. This subtle spot, this zone between beauty and its destruction is tense and expectant; it is a thrilling and dangerous shattering of illusions. JY

66
White Lightning, 1983
Oil on canvas
65 1/2 x 78 1/2

James Rosenquist, born Grand Forks, North Dakota, 1933; lives in Aripeka, Florida

STANDARD

STANDARD

STANDARD

STANDARD
ARD

Ed **Ruscha**

An engaging mix of pop consciousness, California cool, cinematic vision, and automobile culture, Ed Ruscha's paintings at once celebrate and undermine the slick surface of contemporary urban life. An artist who has lived in Los Angeles since 1952, he creates paintings combining words and images in ways that question the reliability of language as a medium of communication. Sometimes he mimics the technicolor backdrops of epic movies, letting an incongruous phrase or statement float disembodied over a brilliant field of sunset orange. Or, he may make a word itself an image, as when he paints the word "wet" over a neutral ground in a cursive script that seems literally drawn in water. Displacing words from their usual contexts, he thrusts us into a topsy-turvy world where no meaning is completely stable.

These *Standard Stations* are vintage Ruscha. Related in part to a series of early works in which the artist provided a deadpan photographic tour of "Some Los Angeles Apartments" or "34 Parking Lots," this set of four serigraphs appears at first to offer a straightforward representation of the ubiquitous California gas station. On second glance, however, it becomes clear that Ruscha is having fun with us. Viewed dramatically from below and fixed with corporate symbols that soar over their roofs like movie marquees, these gas stations become heroic monuments to our culture's massive gas consumption. The repetition of the logo in *Double Standard* suggests that the word has a double meaning—it is not just a brand name, but a comment on the generic corporate architecture that has standardized our urban landscapes. Two versions of the image make reference to food—the rich chocolate tones of *Mocha Standard* and the cocktail olive in *Cheese Mold Standard with Olive* imply a connection between the automobile and our culture's other forms of hedonism.

Like Andy Warhol, an artist with whom he is often compared, Ruscha holds a mirror up to the American way of life. His banal imagery and free-floating puns unhook familiar clichés from their usual moorings, setting them careening across the American landscape. Without either condemnation or approval, Ruscha reveals our fascination with escapism, our focus on the pleasures of consumption, our blindness to a world outside the image defined for us by popular culture. What we do with this information, he seems to suggest, is up to us. EH

67
Standard Station, 1966
Silkscreen,
ed. 4/150
25 1/2 x 40 1/2

Mocha Standard, 1969
Silkscreen,
ed. 26/100
25 1/2 x 40 1/2

Cheese Mold Standard with Olive, 1969
Silkscreen,
ed. 36/150
25 1/2 x 40 1/2

Double Standard, 1969
Silkscreen,
ed. 17/40
25 3/4 x 40 1/4
(Clockwise, from top left)

Ed Ruscha, born Omaha, 1937; lives in Los Angeles

Robert **Ryman**

Contemporary art has perhaps no more subtle poet than Robert Ryman, who reduces paint and painting to quiet but profound essences. Among the great surprises encountered in examining his work is that these essences are expansive rather than limiting, that all his reductions finally lead to enhancements; never have spare white pictures revealed so much.

Ryman arrived in New York in the early 1950s intending to be a jazz saxophonist. He worked as a guard in the Museum of Modern Art, which gave him uninterrupted opportunities to study the traditions and techniques of recent art. He soon became a painter, and from the first Ryman restricted his art to exploring the processes and aesthetics of painting, to formulating conclusions about what is at stake in the age-old activity of applying viscous liquids to prepared surfaces. He wants to know what stroke, saturation, texture, gloss, mark making, restraint, and completion can mean, why they carry wonder, why we care about passages of paint scumbled across a surface. Ryman's inquiry demands abstraction and the restriction of his palette to white; any referential color or hint of subject matter might trigger narrative associations and sidetrack viewers away from the agenda at hand.

Distributor holds its place on the wall like a trophy or shield. Ryman's interests have led him to investigate how pictures are attached to walls, and to incorporate that into their own history; thus the bolts and fasteners used to adhere *Distributor* to the wall are part of its meaning. But it is the imperturbable surface of this painting that is its greatest challenge. Almost Zenlike in purity and concentration, Ryman's brushstrokes accumulate in determined democracy; none seeks special weight, none calls for extra notice. Like sands in an hourglass, they take import from their sheer number. But note the evidences of duration introduced to prevent *Distributor* from being a stultified rendering of an abstract concept. The brown scrim that surrounds the painted area is not equal on all four sides, making the entire image off-center and askew. We observe *Distributor's* lack of surface uniformity, how the build-up of paint can make slight but quite noticeable differences across it. Like some kind of visual haiku, *Distributor* is a call to nuance, a subtle tugging that suggests we slow up a bit, and look. JY

68
Distributor, 1985
Oil on fiberglass with
wood, aluminum
48 x 43

Robert Ryman, born
Nashville, 1930; lives in
New York City

Italo **Scanga**

Italo Scanga emigrated from Italy to the United States in 1947 at the age of fifteen, and, like many before him, brought to his adopted country the legacies and concerns of a homeland lost but never forgotten. In his art, he often harks back to the land of his birth, its extraordinarily rich history, culture, and traditions, recognizing in them much of what he has subsequently become. In works such as *Dux,* Scanga remembers the ambiance of his youth, and through his system of presentation enshrines it in a memorial to memory. In a manner curiously reminiscent of the films of Federico Fellini, *Dux* makes us privy to components of the stupendous tapestry that is Italy, and to its complex historical continuum.

At the heart of *Dux* (the title is Latin for "leader") is its evocation and rendition of Il Duce, Benito Mussolini. When Scanga was growing up in the 1930s in a small town in the province of Calabria (the "toe" in the Italian "boot"), the visage and voice of Mussolini must have been indelibly etched into his consciousness. Mussolini's promise of a return to Italian geopolitical dominance, and his careful and assiduous development of a cult of personality seduced his nation toward eventual ruin. Scanga's presentation of Il Duce, undoubtedly recalled from the endless posters that glorified his rule, emphasizes Mussolini's swagger and blunt and dogged determination, as well as his militaristic posture and aura.

But Mussolini makes up only a part of the fabric of the artist's memory; *Dux* as autobiography is composed of several disparate strands. Also prominent in Scanga's charcoal drawing is an imposing image of a peasant woman wrapped in scarf and shawl. Present too are a pig, bird, and a piece of fruit, which Scanga deploys across the paper without regard for spatial or illusionistic logic. Like a dream, *Dux* comes in disconnected fragments, in fits and starts that compile toward meaning. Scanga exalts these recollections in part by setting them within a hand-modeled and decorated frame, and even more pertinently by the creation of its companion pedestal and glass vase. Per the artist's directions, fresh flowers are placed in this vase in perpetuity, transient votive offerings of beauty to what has been lost along the way. *Dux* is a lyrical souvenir, an altar dedicated to the remembrance of things past. JY

69
Dux, 1981
Charcoal on paper, wood, glass cup
87 x 39 1/2 x 14

Italo Scanga, born Calabria, Italy, 1932; lives in La Jolla, California

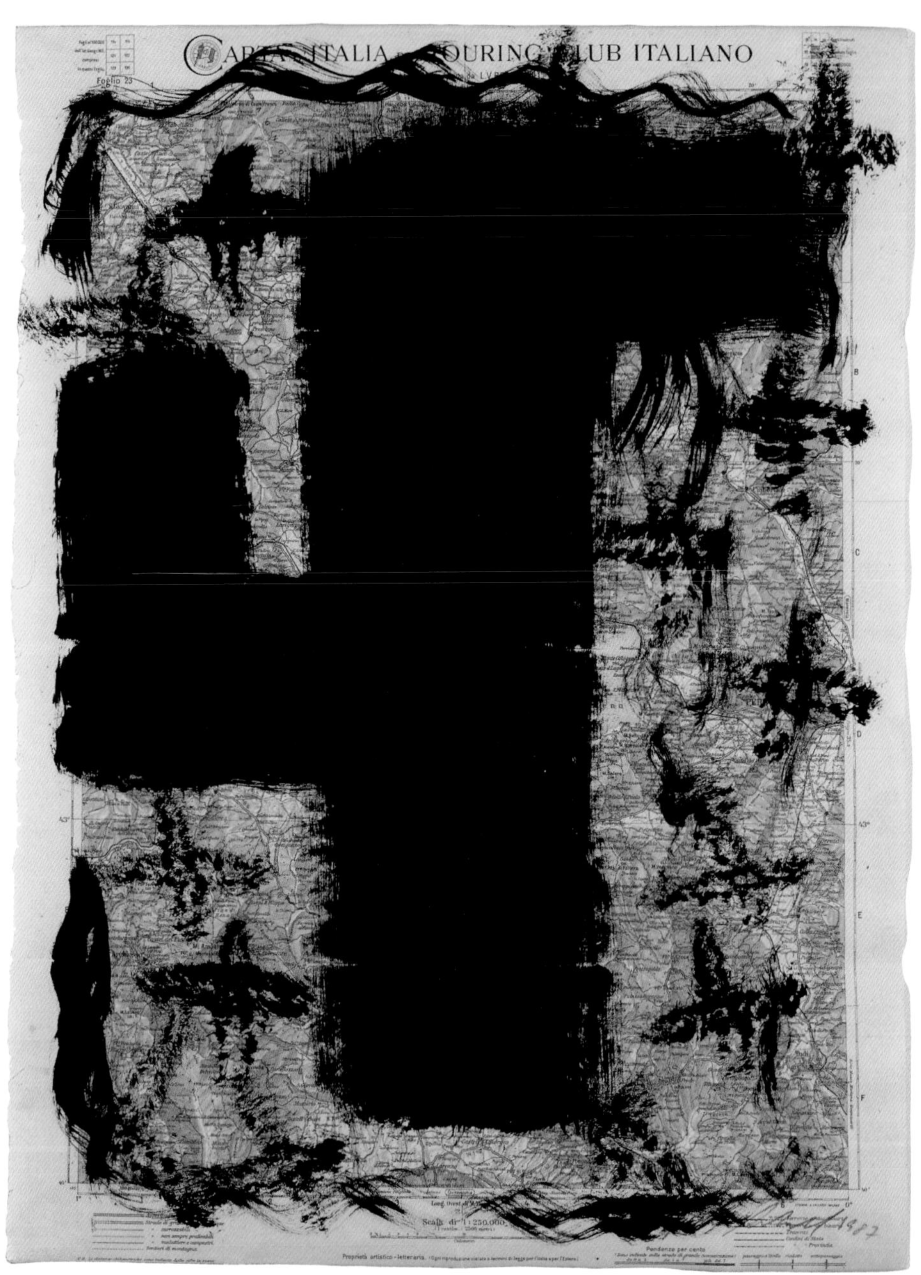
CARTA ITALIA TOURING CLUB ITALIANO
Foglio 23

Julian **Schnabel**

Julian Schnabel's rise to art super-stardom in the 1980s was one of the major stories of that decade. In many ways, his art and his personality seemed to embody much of what characterized that period—a cult of youth, an admiration for brazen aggressiveness, and an aura of big ambition and big money. He represented a sense of open-handed self-indulgence that many read as freedom from the more constrained and intellectual art of the 1970s. Schnabel's huge, colorful, and turbulent canvases were received as transfusions of dynamism and energy, and, whether covered with broken crockery or slathered over black velvet, his imagery promised a return to art with narrative and metaphoric tensions.

Schnabel's gusto and pictorial inquisitiveness are well illustrated in these six ink drawings made over maps of areas of Italy. He recognizes the allure of cartography, how we as viewers will pore over the lovely surfaces of these maps, which were taken from a road volume of the Touring Club Italiano. Maps are both symbols and surrogates for the places and nations they document, and we invest them with a sense of authenticity and mystery. Visions of the Tuscan countryside, sunny inlets and beaches, dusty town squares, the glory that was Rome, and rugged mountainsides covered with vineyards lurk beyond, under, and through Schnabel's manipulations. The paper on which he draws becomes more than just a support or a blank receiver of artistic impulse; it interacts with the artist and viewer, pointing to possibilities and counter-rhythms that inform the total work of art.

Schnabel appropriates and exploits the mystique and contour of Italy, and then covers it with a kind of willful graffiti that risks obscuring and defiling it. This tension and edge of bravura are important components in his art of brinkmanship. Schnabel assuredly seeks the line that separates meaning from chaos, and has no fear of occasionally overstepping it. Indeed, it is precisely in that precarious balancing act where excitement rests that most can be won or lost. His broad swaths of ink seem arbitrary, articulated without too much discrimination, but whether purely abstract or vaguely figurative, they drive their images relentlessly forward to their charged moment of truth. Like a matador's swing of the cape, Schnabel's strokes cull art from danger. There is a thrill in watching just how this bold and risky maneuver is performed, and how the craft of an expert artisan is tested right before our eyes. JY

70
Notes on a Bad Summer, 1987
Gouache on paper map
20 x 15

Julian Schnabel, born New York City, 1951; lives in New York City

Sean **Scully**

One might expect an artist who limited himself to the painting of stripes to have very modest ambitions. For Sean Scully, however, the permutations of the stripe offer a vocabulary with which to explore the whole human condition. Unlike artists such as the late Gene Davis, for whom the precision of a regular field of stripes offered escape from messy reality into a realm of intellectual order, Scully takes his inspiration from the chaos of daily life—gaily colored beach umbrellas, rows of pillars, the shadows that fall from a stand of trees or a set of barred windows.

Eschewing the machinelike exactitude and premeditated approach of some of his colleagues, Scully revels in a makeshift aesthetic. His stripes have uneven edges which blend into each other, and it is often possible to make out traces of earlier compositions below the visible surface. The paintings themselves are pieced together into crazy quilts of horizontal and vertical stripes on panels that butt up against each other or are stacked until they take on a sculptural quality. Scully's colors come from nature: the muted shades of *Over*, for example, bring to mind the rich tones of the earth, perhaps, or the shimmer of the sea or the bright convergence of clouds and sky. The artist has appended one panel of this painting so that it stands out in relief from the others—another reminder of the physical reality of these works.

All of these devices give Scully's art an emotional resonance rarely found in contemporary abstract painting. Speaking with Judith Higgins for *Artnews* in 1985, Scully described his intentions thus: "What I'm trying to do is to use a deliberately elemental structure and set it up so that the paintings have very different rhythms, very different personalities—one may have a kind of intimacy, another a sort of wildness, or a brutality, an ugliness, a lyricism, a brightness, a darkness, a claustrophobic feeling, a powerfully aggressive feeling. In that sense my painting is like figurative art: I'm trying to say something definite rather than seeing how many paintings I can get out of a certain ideal." Thus in Scully's hands, abstraction is a means of enhancing rather than reducing the possible meanings of a work of art. He invites the viewer to engage with his paintings on a variety of levels, offering them to us as tapestries as richly complex as life itself. EH

71
Over, 1985
Oil on canvas
76 1/2 x 65 1/2

Sean Scully, born Dublin, 1945; lives in New York City

Carole **Seborovski**

At its invention early in this century, and for most of its subsequent history, abstract art appeared to its adherents to offer some special transcendent possibilities not to be found in realism or figuration. It was believed that through abstraction, particularly hard-edged abstraction, the tawdry and mundane trappings of reality could be left behind, to be replaced with new and alternative worlds totally of the artist's own making. There, pristine issues could find discourse; there, the life of the mind would replace the tyranny of the eye.

But recent developments indicate that such utopian constructs might have been premature or misapplied. Many artists—and those represented in the Refco Collection include John Armleder, Carroll Dunham, Peter Halley, Sherrie Levine, Holt Quentel, and Tony Tasset—seem much less certain of abstract art's ameliorating possibilities, and are introducing doubt and irony into the arena of contemporary abstraction. Their methods of doing so are varied, but almost every case includes some questioning of the art object's perceived sanctity, reminding us that the work of art is a vehicle, not an arrival.

At first glance, Carole Seborovski's *Grey over Lead* is reminiscent of the moody and introspective late canvases of Mark Rothko. There is a similar confluence of two large pictorial areas, a spare and somewhat ascetic involvement, a conscious reduction of elements, and an attendant narrowing of focus. But any tendency to see in Seborovski the spiritual hopes of Rothko should be amended by closer observation. Seborovski is definitely unconcerned with creating an immaterial or atmospheric effect; in *Grey over Lead*, she accepts the imperfections found in sheet metal, allowing at the top its battered and chipped surface to read through her enamel paint, and at the bottom its bruised metallic history to dictate its appearance.

There is a kind of charming diffidence at work here, a cooperation with materials that avoids imposing solutions upon it. One senses that the present status of this piece of sheet metal is just another stage in its history, that its transformation into art may not be its final stop. Seborovski even indicates that the piece should be adhered directly and unceremoniously to the wall; each corner of *Grey over Lead* is pierced with a nail hole. Through these gestures, in a way, abstraction is reintroduced into the sea of ambiguities that constitute life. Rather than positing transcendental solutions, Seborovski luxuriates in the possibilities of dilemma. JY

72
Grey over Lead, 1985
Enamel on sheet metal
30 x 20 1/2

Carole Seborovski, born San Diego, 1960; lives in New York City

Richard **Serra**

Richard Serra's sculptures are known for their overpowering scale and gravity-defying effects. Huge slabs of Cor-ten steel obviously weighing many tons are set in apparently precarious arrangements, daring the viewer to come too near. However, from up close, or even inside these works (some consist of curving planes that form a navigable cavity), the massive steel walls may begin to seem sheltering rather than threatening.

Having come to prominence in the 1960s, Serra is associated with Minimalism, and like many of his colleagues has eschewed illusionism and metaphor for a kind of visual and intellectual clarity. But among the company of Donald Judd, for instance, whose neatly fabricated boxes explore basic structures, and Carl Andre, whose installations conflate art and real building materials, Serra stands out for the raw emotionalism of his work. His imposing pieces bring the viewer to an uncomfortable awareness of his or her own fragility and vulnerability. It is no wonder then that Serra's work has been controversial, particularly when placed in public settings where casual passers-by unexpectedly come into contact with its uningratiating aesthetic.

Another important characteristic of Serra's sculptures is the way they create an almost architectural space. The viewer is encouraged to move around and through monumental forms which can never be experienced in their entirety from any single point of view. Instead, their relationship to the viewer is constantly shifting as new vistas open and others become closed off. Slowly unfolding in time and space, Serra's slabs and the passages and enclosures they generate must be experienced in the same physical way we come to understand the compartmented areas of our homes and workplaces.

Translated into the two-dimensional space of drawing, the sculpture's physical presence is softened, but the sense of inner strength remains. Building up layers of charcoal or black paint stick so thickly that they become dimensional, the artist creates simple geometric forms which seem to slip at odd angles off the white rectangle of the paper. At times, Serra's drawings suggest rudimentary structures or diagrams, referring back to the architectural concerns of the sculptures. Thus in *Slat* we feel the energy compressed within this opaque black form as it threatens to burst the bounds of the paper on which it rests. Its deep black silhouette becomes a representation of pure mass. For all its inarticulate silence, we sense that *Slat* is defying us to pass by unchallenged. EH

73
Slat, 1986
Paint stick on paper
87 3/4 x 79 3/4

Richard Serra, born San Francisco, 1939; lives in New York City

Cindy **Sherman**

One of the chief messages of advertising is that it is possible to reinvent oneself. This article of clothing, this brand of cologne, even this soft drink, we are insistently told, will somehow transform even the most unprepossessing person into star material. The photographs of Cindy Sherman explore the seductiveness and hidden dangers of this promise. Her work is about masquerade—in each image the artist plays at dress up—adopting the proper costume, pose, and stage props that will transform her into vamp, small town innocent, fairy tale witch, fashion model, winsome schoolgirl. From photograph to photograph, Sherman undergoes a complete and convincing transformation, yet, taken together, the ensemble of images she has created raise questions about the authenticity of any identity.

This is because no role the artist adopts is wholly original. Each has been shaped by the media, embodying the conventions of such genres as B-movies, fashion photography, old master paintings, girlie calendars, and science fiction. In one early body of work, Sherman played the female protagonist in a series of black-and-white *Untitled Film Stills* which were so suggestive of 1950s low-budget movies that many viewers were convinced they had seen the non-existent movie on which the image was based. In her subsequent work, Sherman has oscillated between explicit homage to specific genres and more free-floating amalgams of cultural influences.

This untitled image plays on Western culture's fascination with the exotic East. Drawing aside a set of black curtains which almost seem to transform her body into an armless trunk, this mysterious woman stares out at us with an inscrutable, yet challenging expression. She is clearly an Other, conjuring up an assortment of personas ranging from the fortune teller and the harem girl to the avenging spirit—which have nothing to do with the viewer's direct experience and everything to do with art, film, and popular culture. Thus, the paradox of Sherman's work is that it suggests that the identities we create for ourselves can never really be our own, since they are assembled from a set of fantasies molded by the culture at large. Like the viewer of this image, we may peer behind the curtain, but what we discover there is nothing more than a projection of our own desires. EH

74
Untitled #117, 1983
Color photograph
ed. 4/18
34 3/4 x 24 1/2

Cindy Sherman, born Glenridge, New Jersey, 1954; lives in New York City

Sandy **Skoglund**

The rivalry between photography and painting has been one of the shaping forces in modern art. For much of their mutual history, the two media have managed to coexist by staking out separate realms of accomplishment. While painting claimed for itself the field of illusion and imagination, photography settled into the realm of cold hard fact. Recently, however, artists have attempted to blur these lines, incorporating photography into painting or deliberately subverting the camera's aura of objectivity. Sandy Skoglund is a practitioner of the latter tendency. Her staged photographs are full of obviously artificial props and impossible events. Posing real people in unreal scenarios, she creates hallucinatory nightmare images in which ordinary reality runs amok. Part of the eerie effect of her works derives from our lingering faith in the truth of the photographic image, despite all evidence to the contrary. She demonstrates how photography makes even the most absurd tableaux somehow convincing.

In Skoglund's images, ordinary folks hanging about in their drab homes or offices receive bizarre visitations. A school of enormous goldfish may rain down upon their living rooms, a profusion of huge blue leaves may suddenly grow up among their desks and file cabinets, or, as here, they may be inundated with a pack of electric-green radioactive cats. In order to emphasize the unreality of the scene, Skoglund has painted all the surfaces in this rather depressing tenement apartment a dull gray, while her live characters assume attitudes of total obliviousness to this miraculous event.

Skoglund makes playful reference in her staged photographs to the visual conventions of grade-B horror movies, science fiction, and other pop-culture fantasies. However, beneath this air of humorous absurdity, there lies a deeply submerged awareness of the terrors of modern existence. Her passive protagonists embody a sense of powerlessness that many of us feel in the face of the unimaginable, while their extraordinary predicament suggests the revenge of nature against a disrespectful culture. Meanwhile, the work's title and the neon hue of these fantastic felines make unmistakable reference to the nuclear threat. Photography, with its ability to conflate fact and fiction, an illusion of journalistic veracity with the clearly impossible, adds another layer of perversity to this already demented vision. For Skoglund, imagining is seeing. And, thanks to the camera, seeing is believing. EH

75
Radioactive Cats, 1980
Cibachrome color photograph,
artist's proof 5/10
30 x 40

Sandy Skogland, born Quincy, Massachusetts, 1946; lives in New York City

Haim **Steinbach**

76
together naturally, 1986
Ceramic, wood, formica
24 x 40 x 14 3/4

Haim Steinbach, born Israel, 1944; lives in New York City

The term "Postmodernism" has been stretched to cover a very large variety of contemporary cultural products. It appears in discussions of the eclectic and historicizing tendencies of recent architecture, and in analyses of the performances of pop mega-star Madonna. One hears it invoked to describe the allure of television series like "Dallas" and "Dynasty" as well as the psychology of current political advertising. "Postmodern" has become a catch-all word used to characterize any public form of communication that seems overtly self-conscious and strategic, and that successfully simulates a perceived cultural language without attempting legitimately to represent it.

Haim Steinbach is a postmodern sculptor extraordinaire. He is fascinated with negating the artist's traditional role as object-maker and with how art objects are presented and utilized by their audience. Steinbach did not make the items in *together naturally*; he bought them in a store. His intervention was restricted to their selection, and to the design (not the making) of the pedestal on which they rest. For us, though, the plates and bowls are nonetheless irrevocably altered by Steinbach's manipulation; instead of cursorily examining them as we would if they were arranged in some housewares store, we grant them the incredible aura of significance that resides in any object presented in an art context. These items take their meaning now not from their inherent value, but from their manner of display.

This is not, however, the stuff of cultural anarchy. Steinbach has carefully chosen his plates and bowls with an eye toward maximum visual appeal. The yellow bowls and tan plates can read as yellow circles next to tan bars, creating an abstract picture utilizing the three contrasting shades of brown formica beneath them. A certain (and calculated) paucity of invention causes and/or invites speculations of this order; we understand the mechanics of pristine presentation shown here, and wish to see them aimed at a message of importance. And therein lies Steinbach's sting. He complies with the tactics of display and the vocabulary of advertising only to undercut them, to posit them as degraded and empty. *together naturally* is a tense salvo arguing that in modern culture not only is style preferable to substance, but that we may be losing the power and impetus to distinguish between them. JY

Frank **Stella**

"What you see is what you see." Frank Stella's description in 1964 of his intentions as a painter is one of the most famous art pronouncements of the postwar period. It expresses a radical break both from the highly emotional and expressive work of the Abstract Expressionists who immediately preceded him, and from the earlier spiritual aspirations of abstract painters toward the beginning of the century. Rather than seeking some larger truth or attempting to expose reality's invisible essences through art, Stella espoused the doctrine of formalism, which limits the scope of art to the realm of immediate experience.

For a formalist, art making resembles a chess game, following pre-established rules derived internally from the nature of the artwork itself. Thus, for instance, Stella's work throughout the sixties and seventies (in the 1980s it has changed dramatically) is characterized by a rejection of all the techniques developed by Western artists throughout history to create an illusion of space and movement on the canvas. Instead, Stella treats the painting as a physical object, maintaining the actual flatness of the surface on which he works and allowing the contours of the canvas to generate the abstract lines and shapes he lays over it.

These concerns are clearly evident in this suite of prints from 1971, which present a series of patterns based on the square. Whether he employs a sequence of diagonal lines, a right-angled spiral or a set of inset squares, Stella is careful here that line not create form and that the pattern not break through the surface in an illusion of depth. The colors are deliberately flat, chosen not for their expressive potential but to serve as a means of differentiating each composition. With devices such as these, the artist ensures that the viewer's pleasure in these works will be cerebral rather than emotional.

Throughout his long and remarkable productive career, Stella has assumed the role of the artist as problem-solver, exploring the conundrums presented by the painting as a self-contained object. Yet, despite their aesthetic origins, his works have a playful quality. They offer us a glimpse of a highly logical mind working through a set of formal possibilities with wit, style, and elegance. EH

77
Benjamin Moore Series, 1971
Six lithographs, ed. 10/100
each 16 x 22
(detail)

Frank Stella, born Malden, Massachusetts, 1936; lives in New York City

Donald **Sultan**

The traditional still life exudes a cozy domestic aura, and speaks of stability and refuge from the chaotic outside world. But perhaps because that world is more and more intrusive on our daily existence, still life has fallen on hard times in contemporary art. Donald Sultan is one of the few younger artists to take an interest in this tradition. Working on the cusp between abstraction and recognizable imagery, employing unorthodox materials as well as heavy black oil paint and charcoal, he makes still life articulate the poetry of decay and the morbid beauty of industrial waste.

Lemon and Eggs is one of a series of works in which mealtime staples are transformed into looming iconic presences. Arranged as if in a bowl before us, these ovoid objects threaten to burst out of the paper, and their boundaries blend into each other to create an amorphous mass of deep black. In this work and others from the series, Sultan creates a tension between elegance and decay. With their smoldering black contours, these eggs and lemons have the aura of death about them, speaking to a particularly modern sense of doom. The viewer thinks of blackened factory chimneys, industrial debris, charred wartime remains. One is both attracted and repelled by these images in a manner that parallels our culture's ambivalence toward the promises and ravages of industrialization.

The seductiveness of destruction is a recurring theme in Sultan's work. Along with still lifes, he has created huge paintings of flickering forest fires, train wrecks, and other disasters, literally burning the images out of tar-coated linoleum tiles. These epic paintings serve as counterpart to the more delicate imagery of works like *Lemon and Eggs.* In both cases, the images seem on the verge of disintegration, as if they were about to slip back into some bubbling chaos. Sultan has pointed out that this ambiguity is part of his intention: "I want my paintings to be almost indecipherable," he stated to critic Gerrit Henry for *Artnews* in 1987, "as if the viewer were inside the painting, in the fire, in a state of confusion."

Sultan has often been classed with the Neo-Expressionists who came to prominence during the 1980s and whose work has an emotional quality that contrasts strongly with more cerebral currents in contemporary art. For Sultan, as for other artists of this persuasion, the task of art is not to create order, but to bring to the surface of life the darkening chaos below. EH

78
Lemon and Eggs
August 31, 1987, 1987
Charcoal on paper
60 x 48

Donald Sultan, born Asheville, North Carolina, 1951; lives in New York City

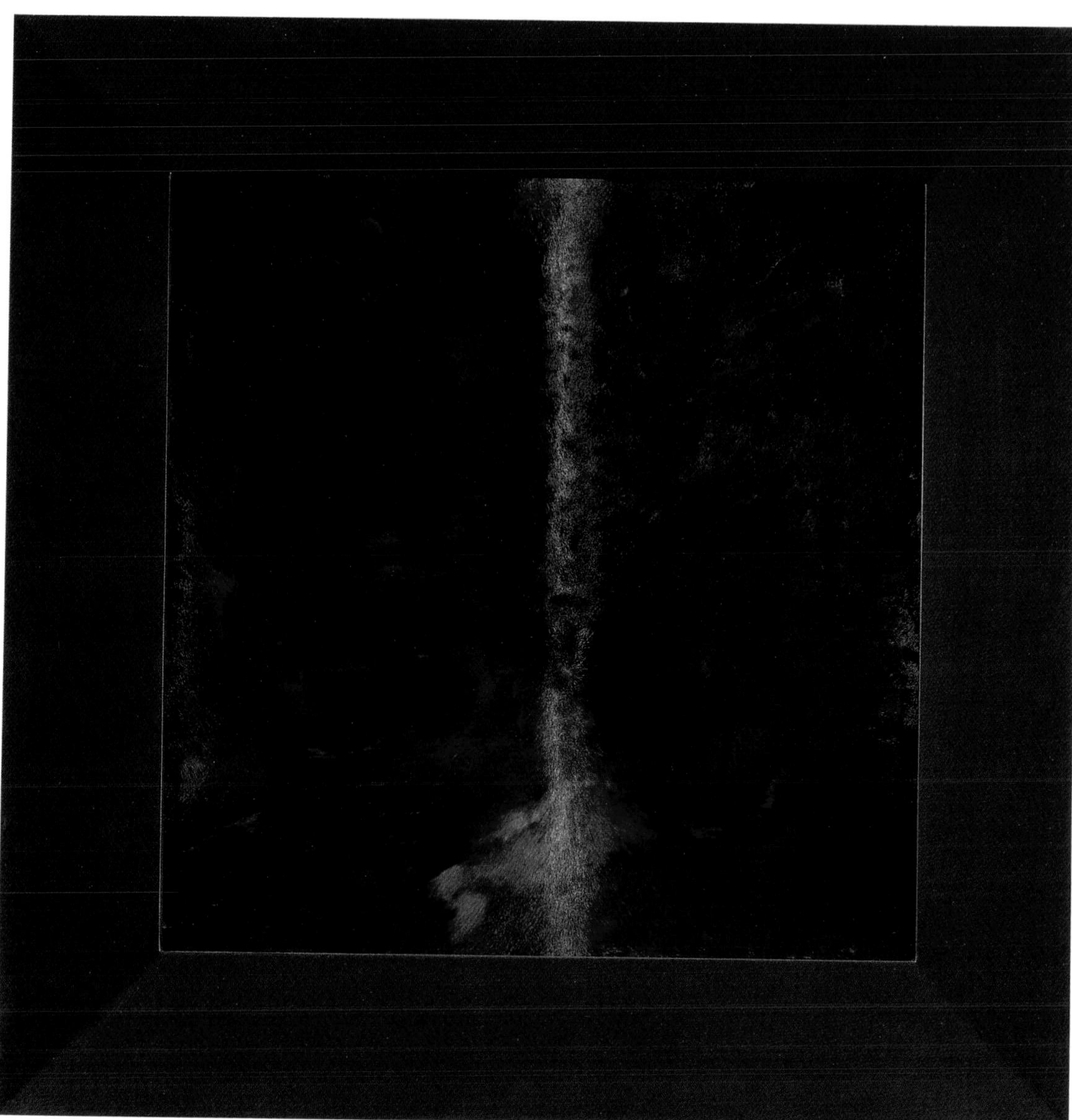

Tony **Tasset**

Tony Tasset's art is a witty, seductive, subtle, and delicate probing of many of the principles constituting contemporary art, particularly those concerning its production and presentation. With the assuredness of an heir and a thorough comprehension of his artistic predecessors, he simultaneously enshrines and undercuts their practices. Tasset elevates to conquer, and while his work never quite descends to parody, he leaves the motives of his sources—and its consumers—partially unmasked.

Domestic Abstraction is one of a series of works that visually mimic some of the semblances and traditions of Minimalism. Enclosed in an immaculate and pristine frame is a field of deep blacks and browns, a restrained area on which the fall of glinting light causes subtle swirls and eddies. At first it might appear that we are confronted with a discreet and circumspect inquiry into a narrow range of pictorial effects, that we are, as with the work of artists such as Brice Marden or Robert Ryman, asked to observe a subtle and expert performance of poetic evocation. But none of their aesthetic feats of prestidigitation were employed to create the surface of *Domestic Abstraction*; it is made of a piece of cowhide Tasset had stretched across its surface.

Removed from the warm body of its source, the hide now drapes a cool institutional wall. Tasset's piece—not a sculpture, not quite a collage, not really akin to painting—positions the art object as a kind of trophy of victory. The fur of an animal is again used in a manner as has long been the custom, to connote human power and dominance. Something that was once wild and had lived according to its own dictates is now tamed and domesticated, not to create coats or shoes, but for a visual prize. Tasset's attitude toward this situation is not that of concerned environmentalist; his interests lie much more in our need to consume these objects than it does in the price some animal paid to create them. Desire is the crucial subtext here, ranging from the near sexual desire we might entertain to stroke the surface of *Domestic Abstraction* to the vague thrill of ownership and ascendancy we enjoy when examining this object. It is an exquisite corpse, and beneath its alluring surface a wide range of aesthetic suppositions are calmly flayed. JY

79
Domestic Abstraction,
1988
Hide, painted wood frame
28 x 28 x 2

Tony Tasset, born Cincinnati, 1960; lives in Chicago

Campbell's
CONDENSED
STOUT HEARTED SOUP
CHICKEN 'N DUMPLINGS
NET WT. 10½ OZ.
SOUP

Campbell's
CONDENSED
Important! Add whole milk
NEW ENGLAND CLAM CHOWDER
NET WT. 10½ OZ.
SOUP

Campbell's
CONDENSED
NET WT. 10¾ OZ.
OLD FASHIONED VEGETABLE
MADE WITH BEEF STOCK
SOUP

Campbell's
CONDENSED
STOUT HEARTED SOUP
NET WT. 11 OZ.
HOT DOG BEAN
TENDER BEANS AND LITTLE FRANKFURTER SLICES
SOUP

Campbell's
CONDENSED
GREAT for GRAVIES and SAUCES!
GOLDEN MUSHROOM
RICH IN SLICED MUSHROOMS
NET WT. 10½ OZ.
SOUP

Campbell's
CONDENSED
NET WT. 10¾ OZ.
GREAT AS A SAUCE, TOO!
CHEDDAR CHEESE
SOUP

Campbell's
CONDENSED
THE ALPHABET SOUP
A B C
VEGETARIAN VEGETABLE
NET WT. 10½ OZ.
SOUP

Campbell's
CONDENSED
Tomato-Beef NOODLE O's
NET WT. 10¼ OZ.
SOUP

Campbell's
CONDENSED
NET WT. 10¼ OZ.
Important! Add whole milk
OYSTER STEW
(WITH GRADE AA BUTTER)
SOUP

Campbell's
CONDENSED
one of the Manhandlers
SCOTCH BROTH
(A HEARTY SOUP)
NET WT. 10¾ OZ.
SOUP

Andy **Warhol**

Sometimes an artistic idea can be so consummately successful that it is difficult to imagine what the world was like before it. It is challenging from our vantage point today to remember what audiences in the 1960s must have made of Andy Warhol's renditions of Campbell's soup cans or his pictures of film stars like Marilyn Monroe. These images are now so deeply ingrained in our culture that it seems it always must have been so. But it was not, and merged with the delight that Warhol's pictorial accessibility gave his first viewers was a decided sense of guilty pleasure that such an endeavor could actually constitute art. Warhol stood at a vanguard arguing for a blurring of the often artificial distinctions between high art and low, between "serious" (which usually meant abstract and complex) and "popular" imagery. With his Pop confreres, Warhol sought an art that took its meaning and resonance from the arena of social dialogue rather than the murky autobiographical areas of personal confession.

He did this with an extraordinarily keen sense of graphic design and an awareness of the aims and tactics of advertising. Warhol had been a successful commercial artist in the 1950s, and was aware of how Campbell's design and promotion departments coordinated color, text, and typeface to maximize product clarity. Although there is not a spoon nor a bowl in sight, Warhol understood that presented to us in this manner, these brightly colored metallic cylinders would always mean soup. An almost primal poetry is operative amidst these promises of tender beans and little frankfurter slices: communication is instant and unambiguous. Although much is uncertain in the modern world, Warhol knew we could be sure that if we were to purchase the object depicted at the upper left of *Campbell's Soup II*, we would find it to contain cheddar cheese soup. And it would be great as a sauce, too. Soup cans and movie stars are part of our public vocabulary; they are the too-often overlooked stuff wherein our social fabric may most fully reveal itself. In these works, Warhol asks us to look at Campbell's soup cans in a manner we would never bother to adopt in a supermarket, sensing that here, at the very spot where we live and consume, is where the values we hold most dear may be playing themselves out. JY

80
Campbell's II, 1969
Ten silkscreens,
ed. 22/250
each 35 x 23

Andy Warhol, born
Pittsburgh, 1928; died in
New York City, 1987

William **Wegman**

81
Fay on Red, 1988
Unique Polacolor II
photograph
24 x 20

William Wegman, born Holyoke, Massachusetts, 1943; lives in New York City

The ongoing and very special collaboration between William Wegman and his Weimeraner Fay could inspire enthusiastic analysis of issues like anthropomorphization and the deep-seated, age-old relationship between humankind and dog. One could posit and reflect on the canon of canine, on the many historical and emotional links that have drawn human and hound together, and how our need for love and companionship has found perfect reciprocation in the animal known as our best friend. But we need only witness Wegman's fond gaze here into the eyes of his Fay, and see with what assuredness that gaze is returned, to know that terms like "pet" and "master" do not sufficiently describe this encounter. Through all the roles and machinations, episodes of high and low comedy, parodies, and riotous send-ups that Fay and her collaborator have created, we sense a delightful bond of love and trust between artist and sitter, imbuing these images with a remarkable conviction.

Wegman was a photographer, draftsman, and video artist when he brought the puppy he named Man Ray into his studio in Long Beach, California, in 1970. Almost immediately, Wegman discovered that he could not keep his dog from participating in his films and stills; Man Ray's irrepressible desire to share the world of his owner was unrelenting. Wegman soon perceived the possibilities therein, and began to investigate the range of Man Ray's theatrical presence. It was inexhaustible. Until his death in 1982, Man Ray became the art world's Rin Tin Tin, an endlessly adaptable and wise actor in inventive and tender scenes. Man Ray was a charmed mirror, play-acting in scenes of touching humanness. The substitution of a dog for a person can cause both comic shock and eerie recognition, emphasize the linkage to aspects of the animal within us, and reveal the often very human qualities of animals.

Fay Ray is heiress to Man Ray's legacy. Wegman has found another stupendously natural performer, this time of the female sex. In *Fay on Red*, she seductively exploits her obvious charms, lying before us unabashedly and unashamedly nude, staring at us with all of the insouciance of some brazen odalisque. Languorous and charged with both humor and sensuality, Fay does what actors everywhere aspire to do—she plays her role with determination and skill. JY

Christopher **Wilmarth**

82
Half Open Drawing, 1971
Glass, cable
24 1/2 x 17

Christopher Wilmarth, born Sonoma, California, 1943; died in Brooklyn, New York, 1987

Throughout history, artists have from time to time sought to capture the elusive poetry of light. J. M. W. Turner's visions of Venice as a blaze of blinding sunlight, Claude Monet's late paintings where form dissolves into limpid pools of color, the Luminists' glowing recreations of that imperceptible line where sea melts into sky, all draw on a Western tradition that equates light with the realm of spirit, truth, and higher consciousness. Sculptors, who deal with tangible objects, have been less concerned with the evocation of light. One exception is Christopher Wilmarth, whose deceptively simple glass and metal constructions have a frosty greenish glow that brings to mind the translucence of the ocean surface or the muted gray of a window streaked with rain. The key to Wilmarth's work is a technique of etching ordinary glass with hydrofluoric acid to bring out the inherent green color of glass. The etching is so shallow it cannot be felt with the fingertips, but its effect is magical, creating a mix of light and color that seems to have no physical substance.

In form, Wilmarth's work has much in common with that of Minimalists such as Donald Judd and Richard Serra. Like them, he limits himself to simple geometric shapes and does not conceal the means by which his sculptures and wall pieces are assembled. In *Half Open Drawing*, for instance, the cable that joins the pair of glass sheets becomes an important part of the composition. It gives the work a poignant sense of tenuous connection which would be lost if the pieces were assembled in a less overt manner. In other works, steel plates are tucked gently behind sheets of glass in such a way that the glass seems to dissolve their boundaries.

However, Wilmarth's is a much softened version of the minimalist aesthetic commonly associated with an aura of industrial manufacture and cool, impersonal rationality. In 1985, Wilmarth remarked to Maurice Poirier in *Artnews* that his work is "really about longing, the impossibility of the ideal, the unattainable." He softens the hard edges of Minimalism, both literally, in his use of etched glass to blend the edges of glass and metal, and metaphorically, in the way the elusive colors and combinations in his work encourage a poetic reading. Thus, although confined to sheets of glass and steel or bronze, Wilmarth's works resonate less with the calculated efficiency of modern industry than the mysterious muffled light of the medieval stained-glass window. Their beauty is as fragile as a passing shadow.
EH

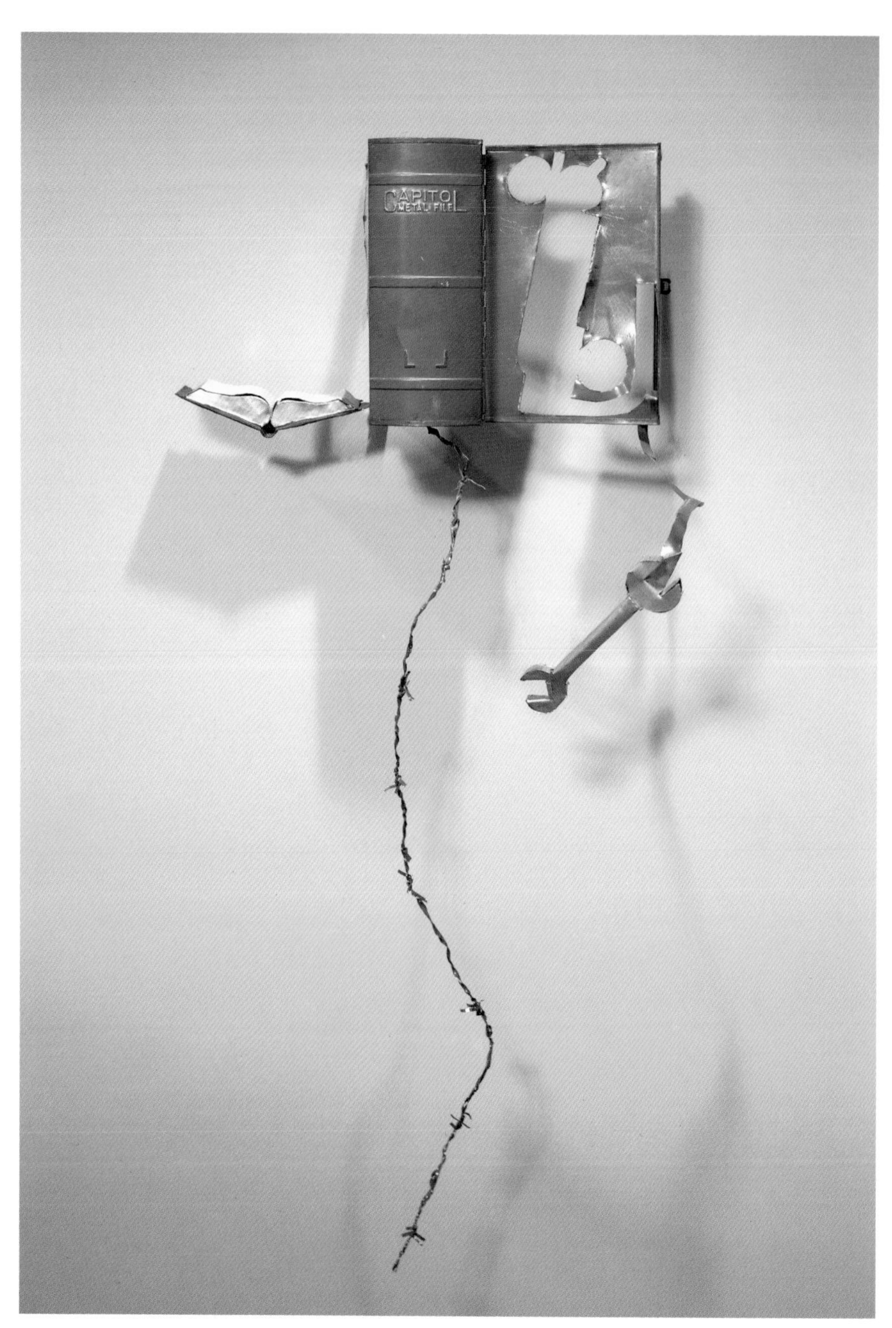
CAPITOL
METAL FILE

Bill **Woodrow**

In the last decades of the twentieth century, there seems no more apt symbol of the tarnished hopes and faded utopian promises of industrialization than a pile of discarded appliances, rusty tools, and broken down machines. Bill Woodrow belongs to a group of British sculptors who have turned the garbage heap of urban civilization into raw material for an art of social commentary. Ingeniously merging the real world and the world of art, Woodrow cuts pieces out of such discards as suitcases, washing machines, and metal file cabinets and uses them to fashion equally ordinary items—guitars, chain saws, sewing machines. He displays the two elements together, leaving the newborn artwork and the original host object linked by a meandering umbilical cord. This simple device allows Woodrow to set up all kinds of paradoxical relationships between "parent" and "child." Sometimes he comments on the opposition between nature and culture in our society by fabricating the metal effigy of a plant or bird out of an old appliance. In other works, he points to the industrial world's patronizing attitude toward "primitive" cultures by fashioning an African mask or totem out of a washing machine or dishwasher.

In yet other cases, the connections are more open-ended. *Capital File,* for instance, in which a wrench, book, and twist of barbed wire sprout from an old metal file, could be interpreted in a variety of ways. On one hand, it offers a meditation on work as an activity, dividing it into intellectual tasks, as represented by the book, and manual labor, suggested by the wrench. A darker reading would take note of the barbed wire and the contrast between the freely offered disclosure suggested by the wide-open book and the withholding of information symbolized by the rigid metal shell of the file.

However we take the particular meanings of these elements, it is clear that Woodrow is interested in creating an object that literally bridges the gap between art and life. His dented and rusty host objects have had another life prior to their reincarnation as Woodrow sculptures, and that history gives the works a resonance that newly minted objects could never have. In the end, the sculptures deliver a mixed message, at once elegiac as they survey the rusty relics of our culture and ironically hopeful as new artifacts arise phoenixlike from the debris of the urban garbage pile. EH

83
Capital File, 1985
Metal file box with acrylic and enamel
46 x 25 1/2 x 11

Bill Woodrow, born Henley, England, 1948; lives in London

The Refco Collection

Dimensions are in inches; height precedes width precedes depth. Catalogue numbers are indicated for works illustrated in this volume.

Pieces marked with an asterisk are owned by Mr. and Mrs. Thomas H. Dittmer.

Vito Acconci
Big Brick, 1984
Aquatint, embossing on paper, ed. 3/24, 71 x 30

Gregory Amenoff
Anima, 1984
Oil on canvas, 80 x 86

Study for Anima, 1984
Ink, oil stick on paper, 18 x 19 1/2

Carl Andre
Aluminum-Copper Alloy Square, 1969
Aluminum, copper; One hundred units, each 1/4 x 7 7/8 x 7 7/8, 1/4 x 78 3/4 x 78 3/4 overall
Cat. no. 1

John Armleder
Untitled, 1987
Oil on canvas with venetian blind, 78 3/4 x 67
Cat. no. 2

Richard Artschwager
Diptych #3, 1967
Formica on wood, 68 x 84 x 4 1/2
Cat. no. 3

Jo Baer
Untitled, 1966-74
Oil on canvas, two panels, each 60 x 84
Cat. no. 4

Jennifer Bartlett
Study for Graceland Mansion,* 1977
Pencil, colored pencil on graph paper, 17 x 22

Graceland Mansion, 1978-79
Drypoint, aquatint, silkscreen on paper, printer's proof 5, 30 x 126

Georg Baselitz
L.R., 1966
Woodcut, ed. 20
17 3/4 x 13 1/2

Lothar Baumgarten
Kulturform, 1977–85
Three black-and-white photographs
each 26 1/2 x 33
Cat. no. 5

Untitled, 1977–85
Three black-and-white photographs
each 26 1/2 x 33

Bernd and Hilla Becher
Watertowers (typology), 1980
Nine black-and-white photographs, each 20 x 16
Cat. no. 6

Lynda Benglis
Rumple, 1977
Chicken wire, cotton, plaster, gesso, gold leaf, 36 x 16 x 7 1/2

Spindle, 1977
Chicken wire, cotton, plaster, gesso, gold leaf, 35 1/2 x 13 1/2 x 6 1/2
Cat. no. 7

Barbara Bloom
Works for the Blind, 1985-89
Seven offset photographs, braille, photographic text, gold leaf, Plexiglas, metal frames, ed. 15, each 32 x 24
Cat. no. 8

Christian Boltanski
Monument, 1988
Photographs, metal frames, electric lights, 77 x 91 overall
Cat. no. 9

Richard Bosman
Mutiny,* 1980-81
Woodcut, ed. 23/36, 18 x 24

Man Overboard,* 1981
Woodcut, ed. 9/17, 27 1/2 x 19

South Seas Kiss,* 1981
Woodcut, ed. 12/31, 16 x 24 1/2

The Kick,* 1981-82
Oil on canvas, 62 x 54
Cat. no. 10

Life Raft, 1983-84
Etching, ed. 24/40, 22 x 29 1/2

Mountaineer, 1986
Oil on canvas, 90 x 60

Bard Breivik
Parts of a Score, 1986
Copper, lead, vine, steel; four units, each 47 x 6 1/2 x 7

Marcel Broodthaers
Museum-Museum, 1972
Two offset lithographs,
ed. 63/100, 33 x 23 1/2

Copie Peint Ecrit, 1972-73
Printing ink, watercolor on paper; three sheets:
11 3/4 x 17 1/2, 11 3/4 x 16 1/4,
14 1/2 x 14
Cat. no. 11

Les Animaux de la ferme, 1974
Two offset lithographs,
ed. 2/20, each 32 1/2 x 24

Daniel Buren
Frieze, Situated Work, 1987
Acrylic, Plexiglas, 132 sheets, each 36 x 36, installed
99 x 2232 x 636 overall
Cat. no. 12

John Cage
(2R)/9 (Where R=Ryoanji), 1983
Pencil on paper, 10 x 19
Cat. no. 13

(3R)/7 (Where R=Ryoanji), 1983
Pencil on paper, 10 x 19
Cat. no 13

(4R)/4 (Where R=Ryoanji), 1983
Pencil on paper, 10 x 19
Cat. no. 13

(13R)/14 (Where R=Ryoanji), 1983
Pencil on paper, 10 x 19
Cat. no. 13

John Chamberlain
Sabine Knights, 1977
Painted and chromium-plated steel, 74 x 30 1/2 x 10 1/2
Cat. no. 14

Christo
Surrounded Islands Project for Biscayne Bay,* 1983
Pastel, charcoal, pencil, crayon, enamel paint, aerial photograph; two parts:
42 1/2 x 65 1/2, 15 1/2 x 65 1/2
Cat. no. 15

Tony Cragg
Dining Motions, 1988
Mixed media, 100 x 200 overall
Cat. no. 16

Enzo Cucchi
La Lupa di Roma, 1986
Aquatint, silkscreen on paper ed. 11/45, three sheets,
each 77 x 38

Agnes Denes
Pyramid Series: 4000 B.C.,* 1973
Ink on orange graph paper,
24 x 30

Jan Dibbets
Four Courts Dublin, 1983
Photo collage and lithographic diptych, ed. 19/25,
each 29 x 31 3/4

Michael Dicerbo
Infernus, 1986
Acrylic on canvas,
54 3/4 x 68 1/4

Jane Dickson
Kiddy Ride, 1984
Oil stick on blue paper; four sheets, each 19 1/2 x 26

Jim Dine
Self Portrait (Red Pony),* 1964
Lithograph, proof, 1st state,
41 x 29

Bathrobe,* 1965
Etching, artist's proof,
17 1/2 x 14

Hearts and a Watercolor,* 1969
Etching, ed. 19/50, 14 x 21

Five Paintbrushes,* 1972
Etching, ed. 73/75, 30 x 40

Bolt Cutters,* 1973
Etching, ed. 25/75, 40 x 30

James Drake
The Illegal, 1987
Steel, charcoal on paper,
87 x 124

Carroll Dunham
Untitled (10/25/85), 1985
Casein, gentian violet on wood veneer, 18 x 13 1/2

Green + Yellow, 1986
Mixed media on elm veneer,
29 3/4 x 24
Cat. no. 17

Nancy Dwyer
Miracle, 1987
Acrylic on canvas, two parts,
each 60 x 75
Cat. no. 18

Christian Eckart
Odyssey (Diptych Variations) #1003, 1987
Formica on plywood, enamel on wood frame, 57 x 162
overall

Dan Flavin
Untitled, 1968
Two fluorescent tubes,
72 x 5 x 4
Cat. no. 19

Untitled (Monument for V. Tatlin), 1968
Fluorescent tubes,
ed. 1/5, 96 x 32 x 4 3/4

Günther Förg
Untitled (Newport), 1988
Acrylic on wood, twelve panels, each
25 3/4 x 19 1/2
Cat. no. 20

Gilbert and George
H.R.H. The Duke of Edinburgh Thinking about the River Thames, 1981
Collaged postcards,
46 1/4 x 28 3/4
Cat. no. 21

Number 10, 1981
Collaged postcards,
32 1/2 x 44 1/2

Ilona Granet
Curb Your Animal Instinct, 1987
Silkscreen on metal, ed. 100, 24 x 24
Cat. no. 22

Are You Men or Mice?, 1988
Silkscreen on metal, ed. 50, 20 x 24

No Cat Calls, 1988
Silkscreen on metal, ed. 100, 24 x 24

Red Grooms
Gertrude,* 1965
Silkscreen in Plexiglas box, ed. 45/46, 19 1/2 x 22 x 11 1/4

Truck,* 1979
Lithograph, ed. 17/75, 24 1/2 x 61

Lorna Doone,* 1980
Lithograph, ed. 9/48, 24 1/2 x 32

Philip Guston
The Wall II, 1975
Oil on canvas, 60 x 88 1/2
Cat. no. 23

Hans Haacke
Alcoa: We Can't Wait for Tomorrow, 1979
Mirror-polished aluminum letters on square aluminum tubing, 9 x 192 x 4 1/2
Cat. no. 24

Peter Halley
Prison with Yellow Background, 1984
Day-glo paint and Rollo-tex on canvas, 60 x 70
Cat. no. 25

Eva Hesse
Untitled, 1960
Watercolor on paper, 10 3/4 x 13 1/2

Sans II, 1968
Polyester resin, 38 x 86 x 6
Cat. no. 26

Jene Highstein
Styrofoam Study,* 1982
Chalk, pastel on paper, 60 x 68 1/2

Jenny Holzer
Untitled (from *Living* series), 1981
Enamel on metal, 21 x 24

Untitled (from *Truisms* series), 1985
Electric sign with yellow diode, ed. 2/5, 5 1/2 x 30 1/2 x 4
Cat. no. 27

Rebecca Horn
Beetles in Conversation, 1988
Mixed media, beetles, 48 x 15 x 5
Cat. no. 28

Ralph Humphrey
Tracks, 1984-85
Acrylic, modeling paste on wood, 54 x 48

Paul Hunter
Untitled, 1987
Charcoal on paper, 26 x 40

Jim Jacobs
Kansas II, 1983
Lacquer on board, 60 x 48 1/2
Cat. no. 29

The Dox Formation II, 1984
Bronze maquette, two pieces, ed. 1/3, 17 x 15 x 6, 12 x 15 x 6

Neil Jenney
Atmosphere, 1985
Oil on panel, 33 x 79 1/2
Cat. no. 30

Luis Jimenez
Bronco, 1978
Two lithographs, ed. 12/35, each 39 1/4 x 28

Jasper Johns
1st Etchings, 1967-68
Six etchings and six photoengravings, hors commerce 4/10, each 25 1/2 x 20 1/2

Grey Alphabet, 1968
Lithograph, ed. 55/59, 50 3/4 x 34

Decoy,* 1971
Lithograph, ed. 49/55, 41 x 29
Cat. no. 31

Land's End, 1979
Lithograph, artist's proof 4/12, 52 x 36

Usuyuki,* 1981
Lithograph, ed. 35/85, 34 1/2 x 50 1/2

Usuyuki II,* 1981
Silkscreen, ed. 35/85, 29 x 48

Donald Judd
Untitled (3 Folded Meters), 1971
Aluminum, ed. 3, three units, each 39 1/2 x 39 1/2

Untitled (Progression), 1979
Aluminum, 6 x 6 x 110 1/2
Cat. no. 32

Ellsworth Kelly
Four Panels,* 1971
Silkscreen, ed. 4/50, 35 3/4 x 62

Anselm Kiefer
Mast, 1984-85
Lead, acrylic, lacquer, emulsion over photograph on board, 41 1/4 x 27 1/2
Cat. no. 33

Komar and Melamid
The Red Flag, 1982-83
Oil on canvas, 96 x 80

Thirty Years Ago 1953, 1982-83
Oil on canvas, 72 x 47
Cat. no. 34

Jeff Koons
Jeff Koons Art Magazine Ads, 1989
Four lithographs, ed. 1/50, each 36 x 28
Cat. no. 35

Willi Kopf
Untitled, 1987
Pasteboard; five units, each 6 1/4 x 12 1/2 x 9 1/2
Cat. no. 36

Jannis Kounellis
Untitled, 1987
Steel, wood, wax, nails,
70 x 71
Cat. no. 37

Barbara Kruger
Untitled (Your Every Wish Is Our Command), 1982
Unique photo montage,
56 x 40 1/2
Cat. no. 38

Untitled (We Are Astonishingly Lifelike), 1985
Lenticular photograph, ed. 3/6,
20 x 20

Untitled (We Decorate Your Life), 1985
Lenticular photograph, ed. 3/6,
20 x 20

Untitled (Your Misery Loves Company), 1985
Lenticular photograph, ed. 3/6,
20 x 20

Untitled (Your Money or Your Life), 1985
Lenticular photograph, ed. 3/6,
20 x 20

Wolfgang Laib
Milkstone, 1988
Marble, milk, 13 x 18 x 2

Susan Laufer
Artifacts Series #8, 1986
Acrylic, mixed media on paper,
50 x 38

Artifacts Series #9, 1986
Acrylic, mixed media on paper,
50 x 38

Bertrand Lavier
Composition No. 7, 1987
Acrylic on sheet metal,
40 x 46 1/2

Annette Lemieux
John Wayne, 1986
Oil on canvas, 72 x 92
Cat. no. 39

Connections, Differences, Paper Dolls, Ash Wednesday, 1988
Four black-and-white photographs, ed. 3/3,
each 27 1/4 x 30 1/2

Sherrie Levine
Untitled (Lead Checks/Lead Chevron: 11), 1988
Casein on lead, 40 x 20
Cat. no. 40

Sol LeWitt
Untitled (Pyramid Wall Drawing), 1986
Ink, pencil wall drawing,
94 x 196 overall

Multiple Asymmetrical Pyramids, 1987
Ink, pencil wall drawing,
110 x 341 overall
Cat. no. 41

Roy Lichtenstein
*Brushstroke,** 1965
Silkscreen, ed. 277/280, 23 x 29

*Still Life with Figurine and Pearls,** 1974
Silkscreen, ed. 79/100, 47 x 38

*Nude in the Woods,** 1980
Woodcut, artist's proof 8/13,
40 x 36

Donald Lipski
Building Steam #243, 1984
Conveyor belt, 41 x 11 x 18

Xalupax, 1985
Mixed-media installation,
variable dimensions
Cat. no. 42

Richard Long
Mud Foot Circle, 1985
River Avon mud on paper laid on board, 88 x 79
Cat. no. 43

Robert Longo
*Frank,** 1982-83
Lithograph, ed. 18/28, 68 x 39

Cindy, 1984
Lithograph, ed. 37/38, 68 x 39

Eric, 1984
Lithograph, ed. 20/38, 68 x 39

Gretchen, 1984
Lithograph, ed. 31/38, 68 x 39

Anne, 1985
Lithograph, ed. 37/38, 68 x 39

Edmund, 1985
Lithograph, ed. 13/38, 68 x 39

George Lorio
Untitled, 1986
Gold leaf, painted wood,
16 x 8 x 7

Interlock, 1987
Painted wood, 6 x 7 x 7

Mark Luyten
Intermezzo, 1987
Mixed media on paper,
59 1/2 x 39
Cat. no. 44

Intermezzo, 1987
Mixed media on paper,
59 1/2 x 39

Robert Mangold
A Square and a 90 Degree Arc with Three Rectangles (Red), 1977
Acrylic, pencil on masonite,
20 x 42
Cat. no. 45

Five Color Frame, 1985
Woodcut, ed. 52/200,
25 x 21

Robert Mapplethorpe
Andy Warhol, 1986
Photograph, ed. 5/10,
27 1/2 x 24 1/4
Cat. no. 46

Brice Marden
#1, 1972
Lithograph, ed. 2/42,
26 x 19

#2, 1972
Lithograph, ed. 2/48,
26 x 19

#3, 1972
Lithograph, ed. 7/40,
26 x 19

#4, 1972
Lithograph, ed. 45/46,
26 1/4 x 19 1/4

#6, 1972
Lithograph, ed. 2/46,
26 x 19

Focus (I-V),* 1979-80
Etching, aquatint, ed. 12/75,
five sheets, each 15 x 11

Couplet Painting Study III, 1987-88
Ink on paper, 22 x 10 1/4
Cat. no. 47

Agnes Martin
*Untitled I,** 1981
Acrylic, pencil on canvas,
72 x 72

Untitled II, 1988
Acrylic, pencil on canvas,
72 x 72
Cat. no. 48

Allan McCollum
Surrogates, 1983
Cast hydrocal, enamel paint;
twenty units,
variable dimensions
Cat. no. 49

Ann McCoy
*The Night Sea,** 1978
Hand-colored lithograph,
two sheets, ed. 17/30,
each 65 1/4 x 34 1/4

Annette Messager
Mes Voeux, 1988
Black-and-white photographs,
strings, 35 1/2 x 19 3/4

Robert Morris
Golden Memories, 1963
Lead, wood, metal, gold-painted rope,
5 1/2 x 28 1/4 x 7

Untitled, 1973
Graphite on paper,
35 x 46
Cat. no. 50

Blind Time III, 1985
Graphite on paper,
38 x 50

Elizabeth Murray
#1, 1986
Lithograph, ed. 16/59,
22 x 31

Blue Body, 1987
Lithograph, ed. 22/70,
47 3/4 x 31 1/2

Bruce Nauman
Symptoms, 1984
Acrylic, pastel on paper,
49 x 45

Double Poke in the Eye II, 1985
Neon, aluminum, ed. 13/40,
24 x 36 x 6 1/4
Cat. no. 51

Claes Oldenburg
*Teabag,** 1972
Lithograph, ed. 72/150,
38 x 30

*Soft Fireplug, Inverted,** 1973
Lithograph, ed. 100/100,
40 x 30 3/4

*Picasso Cufflink,** 1974
Color lithograph,
artist's proof 11/15,
36 x 27

*Chicago Stuffed with Numbers,** 1977
Lithograph, ed. 77/85,
47 1/2 x 30 1/2

Blinky Palermo
Blue Triangle, 1969
Original drawing with
handpainting, cardboard
stencil, paint tube, brush,
cardboard box, ed. 24/50,
variable dimensions
Cat. no. 52

Giulio Paolini
Intervallo, 1974
Plaster, two units,
each 38 1/2 x 21 x 4
Cat. no. 53

Philip Pearlstein,
*Sphinx,** 1979
Aquatint, ed. 41/41,
28 1/2 x 40 1/2

A. R. Penck
Untitled, 1982
Oil on cardboard,
70 3/4 x 90 1/2
Cat. no. 54

Robert Peterson
*Chart Series, Sunday, March 27,** 1977
Lithograph, ed. 4/50,
37 x 24

Sylvia Plimack-Mangold
Before Painting on the Tape Color, 1977
Acrylic on canvas, 30 x 36

Winterset, 1981
Oil on canvas, 60 x 80
Cat. no. 55

Sigmar Polke
Untitled, 1978
Egg tempera on black-and-white photograph,
24 1/2 x 36 1/2
Cat. no. 56

Lottoschein, 1983
Acrylic, wood, fabric,
50 3/4 x 45

Richard Prince
Waves, Bangs, Palms, 1987
Ektacolor photograph,
86 x 47
Cat. no. 57

Garnett Puett
EM II, 1987
Wax, steel, wood, glass case,
24 3/4 x 13 x 13
Cat. no. 58

Martin Puryear
Endgame, 1985
Painted pine,
65 x 62 x 3 3/4
Cat. no. 59

Holt Quentel
Green Cross, 1989
Latex, canvas, rope,
84 x 84
Cat. no. 60

Arnulf Rainer
*Untitled (Übermalte Radierung),** 1961-64
Oil, oil crayon, ink, watercolor over etching, 14 x 19 3/4

Body Language (Körpersprache), 1971
Crayon, oil, pencil on photograph, 19 3/4 x 23 1/4
Cat. no. 61

Robert Rauschenberg
*Accident,** 1963
Lithograph, ed. 15/29, 41 x 29

*Breakthrough I,** 1964
Lithograph, ed. 4/20, 41 1/2 x 30

Visitation I, 1965
Lithograph, ed. 8/42, 30 x 22

Booster, 1967
Lithograph, silkscreen, ed. 37/38, 72 x 36
Cat. no. 62

Gamble, 1968
Lithograph, trial proof 3/5, 41 1/2 x 28

*Glacial Decoy I,** 1979
Lithograph, ed. 8/28, 31 1/2 x 48

*Glacial Decoy II,** 1980
Lithograph, ed. 4/25, 56 1/2 x 39

Charles Ray
Ink Drawing, 1988
Mixed media, 50 1/2 x 43

Edda Renouf
Furrows–Sunrise, 1987
Oil pastel on paper, 22 1/4 x 23 1/4

Richard Rezac
Untitled (Laurel Shelf), 1988
Cast bronze, wood, 16 1/2 x 20 1/2 x 7 1/2
Cat. no. 63

Gerhard Richter
Abstract Painting 584-1, 1985
Oil on canvas, 69 x 98 1/2
Cat. no. 64

14.3.86, 1986
Oil on paper, 32 1/2 x 44 1/2

Tim Rollins and K.O.S.
By Any Means Necessary, 1986
Silkscreen on bookpage, ed. 250, 4 1/4 x 6 3/4

*The Scarlet Letter–Pearl,** 1986-88
Acrylic, watercolor, bistre on bookpages on linen, 24 x 36
Cat. no. 65

James Rosenquist
*Spaghetti and Grass,** 1965
Lithograph, artist's proof, 27 1/2 x 27

Rolldown, 1965-66
Lithograph, color trial proof 3, 38 x 29

*Off the Continental Divide,** 1973-74
Lithograph, ed. 10/43, 42 x 78

Balcony, 1979
Lithograph with mirror, artist's proof 7/12, 22 3/4 x 31

*Chambers,** 1983
Lithograph, ed. 23/25, 30 x 47 1/2

*White Lightning,** 1983
Oil on canvas, 65 1/2 x 78 1/2
Cat. no. 66

The Kabuki Blushes, 1986
Lithograph, monoprint, ed. 8/59, 39 x 41 1/2

Erika Rothenberg
7 Hours, 10 Minutes A Day, 1987
Acrylic on canvas, 50 3/4 x 66 3/4

Susan Rothenberg
Untitled (May #3), 1979
Etching, printer's proof I, 23 3/4 x 17 1/2

Puppet, 1983
Woodcut, ed. 22/25, 70 x 37

Ed Ruscha
*Standard Station,** 1966
Silkscreen, ed. 4/150, 25 1/2 x 40 1/2
Cat. no. 67

*Cheese Mold Standard with Olive,** 1969
Silkscreen, ed. 36/150, 25 1/2 x 40 1/2
Cat. no. 67

*Double Standard,** 1969
Silkscreen, ed. 17/40, 25 3/4 x 40 1/4
Cat. no. 67

*Mocha Standard,** 1969
Silkscreen, ed. 26/100, 25 1/2 x 40 1/2
Cat. no. 67

Robert Ryman
Untitled, 1969
Acrylic on featherboard on fiberglass, 18 x 18

Six Aquatints, 1975
Six aquatints, ed. 20/50, each 36 x 36

*Distributor,** 1985
Oil on fiberglass with wood, aluminum, 48 x 43
Cat. no. 68

Italo Scanga
Dux, 1981
Charcoal on paper, wood, glass cup, 87 x 39 1/2 x 14
Cat. no. 69

Julian Schnabel
Notes on a Bad Summer, 1987
Gouache on paper map,
20 x 15
Cat. no. 70

Notes on a Bad Summer, 1987
Gouache on paper map,
20 x 15

Notes on a Bad Summer, 1987
Gouache on paper map,
20 x 15

Notes on a Bad Summer, 1987
Gouache on paper map,
20 x 15

Notes on a Bad Summer, 1987
Gouache on paper map,
20 x 15

Notes on a Bad Summer, 1987
Gouache on paper map,
20 x 15

Sean Scully
Over, 1985
Oil on canvas,
76 1/2 x 65 1/2
Cat. no. 71

Carole Seborovski
Grey over Lead, 1985
Enamel on sheet metal,
30 x 20 1/2
Cat. no. 72

Parallel Crossed Bands–Second Version, 1987
Charcoal on paper,
8 3/4 x 7 3/4

Vertical Bands–Charcoal Edge, 1988
Graphite, charcoal on paper,
12 3/4 x 7 3/4

*Drop,** 1989
Charcoal, ink, collaged paper, bark,
18 3/4 x 15

Richard Serra
Clara Clara V, 1983-84
Oil stick on paper,
32 1/4 x 52 3/4

Slat, 1986
Paint stick on paper,
87 3/4 x 79 3/4
Cat. no. 73

Joel Shapiro
Untitled, 1975
Charcoal on paper,
38 x 49 3/4

Untitled #1, 1985
Woodcut, ed. 32/40,
12 x 8 3/4

Untitled #2, 1985
Woodcut, ed. 19/44,
19 1/2 x 24

Untitled #3, 1985
Woodcut, ed. 32/41,
17 x 13 1/4

Cindy Sherman
Untitled #91, 1981
Color photograph, ed. 9/10,
24 x 48

Untitled #95, 1981
Color photograph, ed. 3/10,
24 x 48

Untitled #102, 1982
Color photograph, ed. 3/10,
49 x 24

Untitled, #112, 1982
Color photograph, ed. 10
45 x 30

Untitled #116, 1982
Color photograph, ed. 10/10,
44 1/2 x 29 1/2

Untitled #117, 1983
Color photograph, ed. 4/18,
34 3/4 x 24 1/2
Cat. no. 74

Untitled #120, 1983
Color photograph, ed. 15/18,
34 1/2 x 21 3/4

Sandy Skoglund
Radioactive Cats, 1980
Cibachrome color photograph,
artist's proof 5/10, 30 x 40
Cat. no. 75

Jeanette Pasin Sloan
*Silver Bowls,** 1978
Lithograph, ed. 13/50,
29 1/2 x 40

Alexis Smith
Jane Doe, 1985
Mixed media on canvas,
three parts, 29 1/4 x 70 1/4
overall

Haim Steinbach
together naturally, 1986
Ceramic, wood, formica,
24 x 40 x 14 3/4
Cat. no. 76

Frank Stella
Benjamin Moore Series, 1971
Six lithographs, ed. 10/100,
each 16 x 22
Cat. no. 77

The Butcher Came and Slew the Ox (No. 8), 1984
Silkscreen, lithograph, linocut,
handpainting, collage
ed. 21/60,
57 8/10 x 53 3/10

Donald Sultan
Lemons , 1985
Four aquatints,
ed. 9/10, each 63 x 49

Still Life with Lemons, 1986
Three photolithographs,
aquatint, ed. 10/45,
each 24 1/2 x 21

Lemon and Eggs August 31, 1987, 1987
Charcoal on paper, 60 x 48
Cat. no. 78

Tony Tasset
Domestic Abstraction, 1988
Hide, painted wood frame,
28 x 28 x 2
Cat. no. 79

Wayne Thiebaud
Pie Rows (from *Delights* portfolio),* 1964
Etching, aquatint, artist's
proof, 4 x 5

David True
Promises Kept, 1986
Acrylic on canvas, 50 x 72

James Turrell
Deep Sky, 1984
Seven aquatints, ed. 12/45,
each 21 x 27

Juan Usle
The Book of Landscapes (1), 1987-88
Watercolor on paper, 17 x 11

The Book of Landscapes (2), 1987-88
Watercolor on paper, 17 x 11

The Book of Landscapes (3), 1987-88
Watercolor on paper, 17 x 11

Liz Ross Vahlsing-Southern
Os-113, 1986
Oil on canvas, 72 1/2 x 86

John Van Alstine
Go Round, 1983
Charcoal on paper, 30 x 22

D.T.'s (Diagonal Tendencies), 1984
Pastel on paper, 42 x 29 1/2

Drastic Measures, 1984
Pastel on paper, 42 x 29 1/2

Luna, 1985
Charcoal on paper, 30 x 22

Totem, 1985
Pastel on paper, 44 x 30

Ger Van Elk
Sheepcorner, 1984
Enamel paint on photograph, 67 x 69 1/2

Naomi Wakesberg
Oriel Suite III, 1979
Acrylic on paper, 22 x 30

Franz Erhard Walther
Weg Innen Aussen, 1966
Mixed media on paper, 8 1/4 x 11 3/4

Kurz vor der Daemmerung, 1967
Mixed media on paper, 8 1/4 x 11 3/4

Sammelobject (Neun), 1967
Mixed media on paper, 8 1/4 x 11 3/4

Standstellen, 1967
Mixed media on paper, 8 1/4 x 33 1/2

Annaeherung Schritte Seitwaerts, 1968
Mixed media on paper, 8 1/4 x 11 3/4

Green Departure Point, Black Volumes, 1984
Cotton and wood, 36 x 50 x 12

Warhol, Andy
Marilyn, 1967
Feldman-Schellmann 22, Wunsche 10
Silkscreen, 36 x 36

Marilyn,* 1967
Feldman-Schellmann 24, Wunsche 7, ed. 243/250, Silkscreen, 36 x 36

Marilyn, 1967
Feldman-Schellmann 25, Wunsche 9, ed. 212/250, Silkscreen, 36 x 36

Marilyn, 1967
Feldman-Schellmann 27, Wunsche 13, ed. 219/250, Silkscreen, 36 x 36

Marilyn, 1967
Feldman-Schellmann 28, Wunsche 15, ed. 91/250, Silkscreen, 36 x 36

Marilyn, 1967
Feldman-Schellmann 29, Wunsche 12, ed. 91
Silkscreen, 36 x 36

Marilyn, 1967
Feldman-Schellmann 30, Wunsche 14, ed. 91/250, Silkscreen, 36 x 36

Campbell's II, 1969
Ten silkscreens, ed. 22/250, each 35 x 23
Cat. no. 80

White Brick Wall, 1976-86
Six stitched gelatin silver prints, 33 x 28

William Wegman
On Lee Street Pond, 1984
Three color photographs, each 15 x 15

Judith, 1987
Unique Polacolor II photograph, 24 x 20

Fay on Red, 1988
Unique Polacolor II photograph, 24 x 20
Cat. no. 81

Gerrhino, 1988
Unique Polacolor II photograph, 24 x 20

Raingear, 1988
Unique Polacolor II photograph, 24 x 20

William Wiley
Hides,* 1972
Lithograph, printer's proof II, 33 1/4 x 46 1/4

Hides,* 1972
Monoprint on chamois with hand painting, 26 3/4 x 31 1/2

Christopher Wilmarth
Half Open Drawing, 1971
Glass, cable, 24 1/2 x 17
Cat. no. 82

Bill Woodrow
Capital File, 1985
Metal file box with acrylic and enamel, 46 x 25 1/2 x 11
Cat. no. 83